*He able to do exceedingly abundantly
above all that we ask or think,
according to the power that works in us.*
Ephesians 3:20

Developing Faith for the

Working of Miracles

Miracles

How to Believe for the Impossible

Jennifer LeClaire

Unless otherwise noted, Scripture quotations are taken from the New King James version of the Bible.

Developing Faith for the Working of Miracles: How to Believe for the Impossible

Copyright © Jennifer LeClaire 2013

Published by Jennifer LeClaire Ministries
P.O. Box 3953
Hallandale Beach, Fla. 33008
305.467.4284
www.jenniferleclaire.org

Dedication

This book is dedicated to my parents, who always believed in me even when the supernatural looked impossible. Glory be to God.

Table of Contents

PREFACE

It was one of those unforgettable church services. The glory of God seemed tangible. The gifts of the Spirit were flowing. Jesus was healing some people from hurts and wounds, delivering others from demonic bondages, and encountering still others with His wondrous love. As I watched the Holy Spirit sweep through the sanctuary, it was almost as if I was on top of a mountain looking down. My eyes captured miraculous moments in time that have stayed with me even until now. Lives were literally being changed. People would never be the same.

Suddenly, I heard the Lord say, "My people don't see this too often." When I asked Him why, He was quick to answer: "Because they don't really want to."

I was shocked. What did He mean, "Because they don't really want to"? What Bible-believing Christian doesn't want to see signs, wonders and miracles? What Spirit-filled saint doesn't want to see gifts of healing and prophecy flowing? What blood-bought soul doesn't want to see revival? What did God mean, "Because they don't really want to?"

I was shocked. Yet I know God doesn't lie. And I also know from practical experience that God's people don't see the mighty moves of His Spirit that I was witnessing too often. In other words, the supernatural isn't natural to us. I have visited plenty of churches where dry liturgy, even in supposedly Spirit-filled congregations, reigns. I have visited too many churches where the pastor schedules everything—from introductions to praise and worship to the message to the altar call to the offering to the benediction—right down to the second. There's nothing wrong with an order of service as long as you are willing to abandon it when God shows up. But too many stick to rigid schedules that effectively shut out any move of the Spirit. Indeed, I have visited too many churches where religion quenches the Holy Ghost. He wants to move. But we won't let Him. We want to get home to the chicken in the oven and watch football.

What's going on? There are many little foxes working to spoil the vine, from apathy to compromise to lukewarmness to seeker-friendly pastors to all manners of sin to unbelief—or just not believing long enough. I blame these little foxes for robbing people's hunger and thirst to see a true move of the Spirit. Sure, they may agree with the concept of revival or renewal or spiritual awakening but they aren't willing to press in to that possibility, again, because of apathy or compromise or lukewarmness or seeker-friendly pastors or various kinds of sin or unbelief—or just not believing long enough.

As I pondered what the Lord had dropped into my spirit—"Because they don't want to"—the Holy Ghost spoke again. This time, He offered me a key that would open the door to greater manifestations of His presence: "You have to stir up the hunger before you can stir up the anointing." In other words, the anointing responds to our faith. God is always looking for someone to bless—someone who has the faith to believe to receive.

Not completely content with His answer, I pressed in and asked God another question: "How do you stir up the hunger?" I waited with expectation to hear His advice because I want to see God pour out His Spirit over the Body of Christ. So I waited for His answer and He was faithful to reveal the mystery.

"By showing them what's possible…"

With that in mind, my goal with this book is to show you what's possible—the miraculous. I want to stir up your hunger so faith will arise and you can receive what you need from God—even things you once thought were impossible. God wants to see your dreams come true. God wants you to see the miraculous manifest in your life. God wants to give you something that you can only receive from Him by faith. God wants to do what the world says is impossible—but what the Word says is possible. All you have to do is believe.

Whether you've been believing God for decades or you are trying to build faith to believe—and whether you are believing for financial breakthrough, relationship restoration, healing, wisdom, peace—or anything else in line with God's will—I pray this book will help you develop the faith for the working of miracles in your life.

1

Encountering the God of Miracles

needed a miracle. I was in an impossible situation, sitting in a county jail, falsely accused of a crime I didn't commit. I was denied bail three times. Prosecutors were seeking a five-year prison sentence. My high-dollar defense attorneys—who had initially promised me I had nothing to worry about; that they would clear up this "paperwork problem"—gave up on the case. Suddenly, their expert legal advice was to cut a plea deal for less time and hope for the best. I needed a miracle. I was facing an impossible situation. Although I had plenty of money at the time, money couldn't justify me. Money couldn't vindicate me. Money couldn't prove my innocence. I was set up. Only God could help me now.

I had lost a lot already and I had a lot more to lose. About a year earlier, my husband had abandoned me for a woman just more than half his age in a Third World country. He started a new family and never looked back. I was left alone with a two-year-old baby. No alimony. No child support. He simply left on a two-week business trip to Latin America one day never to return. Despite the devastation—and despite being angry with a God I didn't truly know—I had managed to climb the corporate ladder in the midst of my personal devastation. I had a large contract providing editorial services to a major broadcast company's web site. I was getting my life back together one step at a time—until suddenly my past came back to haunt me.

Let's rewind seven years so you can see how God was setting me up for a series of miracles even before I got saved. It all started when I was forced to call the police during an argument with my then-fiancé (who I later married and who later abandoned me and my daughter). He came home from work angry. I had never seen him so angry. I had no idea what was wrong but he was on a warpath. He threw a bowl of macaroni at me as I was running into the bedroom to lock the door behind me. I warned him to calm down or I would call 911. He demanded that I open the door. When I did, he tried to wrestle the phone from my hands. Because my nails were long, he ended up with scratches on his arms from the tussle. Of course, the bruises he left on my wrists wouldn't show up until the next day.

www.jenniferleclaire.org

I finally managed to break free and call 911. This was just after the O.J. Simpson trial, so the police were hyper-focused on domestic violence. County rules demanded that someone go to jail if the police were called. Of course, I didn't know all this. I just wanted my fiancé to calm down and I figured calling the police was my last and best option considering how scared I was. When the police arrived and put my future Mormon husband in handcuffs I began to plead with them not to take him. I didn't want him to go to jail. I just wanted him to calm down. The female officer warned me to, "Shut up or I'll say you hit me!"

Of course, at the time I probably looked like someone who would have hit a cop. I had a partially shaved head, a black strip of hair hanging in front of my eyes, several tattoos and an eyebrow piercing. But I never hit a cop. My biggest mistake was that I naively opened my mouth and incredulously said, "You can't do that!" I was young and naïve. I had no idea there were dirty cops out there with authority issues and inflated egos. This manly female cop took exception to my incredulous statement and decided to show me who was in charge. She grabbed me and slammed me against the police car. She read me my rights as she charged me with battery on a law enforcement officer and resisting arrest with violence. Two felonies. She carted me off to jail, but not before roughing me up and leaving me with bruises all over my body as I struggled, hands cuffed behind my back, to protect myself from the rapid-fire blows.

That event sent me spiraling into a deep depression for which I ended up taking an anti-depressant called Paxil. My attorney sent me to a psychiatrist hoping he would help build a defense that I was "temporarily insane." It was a lie, but because I was young and naïve and scared, I went along with it to avoid jail time. I wasn't temporarily insane at all—a corrupt cop set me up. Yet the psychiatrist created a false diagnosis and prescribed me anti-psychotic drugs. The drugs kept me in near comatose state for several days. I realized that if I continued down that path I would indeed end up in a mental hospital.

I was still a mess so I continued taking the anti-depressant. But I fired the dishonest attorney who sent me down this dangerous path. I decided to represent myself before the judge. I pled "no contest" to the charges. It was the cop's word against my word and legal counsel had previously advised me that I am likely go to prison if I tried to fight it. I agreed to two years of probation and community service. I completed the community service and set out to transfer my probation as my fiancé was called on a permanent assignment in a city three hours away. I actually took my mother into the probation office with me to request the transfer so that I had a witness. The transfer was granted. I gave the probation officer my new address and was told that someone would contact me there once the paperwork was filed.

Upon arriving in the new city, we immediately married and within a few months I was pregnant with our daughter. Memories of the past began fading away. I went on with my life and never looked back—until my husband abandoned me. It was my divorce attorney who turned up a warrant for my arrest that was nearly seven years old. Due to an administrative oversight, the court never transferred my probation to the new city. Despite the fact that the government had my address and my social security number—and despite the fact that I went into a courthouse for a marriage license and into a government building to apply for Medicaid for the pregnancy—no government agency even flagged me.

It was only as I was filing divorce papers that my attorney found the warrant. I'll never forget her frantic phone call telling me to hire a criminal defense attorney immediately and not to return to my home. The sentence for violating probation was five years in prison. My daughter was almost three years old at that time. If convicted, she would be eight years old before I would see her again.

After staying in a hotel for two weeks, a Colombian family that had recently befriended me leased an apartment in their name so I would have a safe haven while I secured legal representation. Soon that relationship turned strangely sour. These Colombians started stealing money from me. They were driving my car as their own. And they were making offers to have my ex-husband killed for $5,000. Fearful, I contacted an old friend who came to my rescue. He moved me to another city in the middle of the night with a few belongings.

Finally, things began to settle down. I hired an attorney and laid out a $15,000 retainer. The attorney assured me he could get the whole thing dismissed with a little community service. It was a respected law firm with a strong track record in wrongful criminal charges. I believed them. What I didn't count on was my maid dropping the dime on me just days before I relocated to New York City to be closer to my editorial assignment.

The maid agreed to pack up my goods for $300. But when the job was done, she wanted double that. I refused to pay her the extra money because she was taking advantage of me and I was tired of being wronged. The next thing I knew, cops were beating down my door in the middle of the night. It seems *America's Most Wanted* was in town. She turned me in for the reward money. I was arrested and taken to a local jail before being transferred to another city in shackles. It was humiliating.

God's Miracle-Working Power Manifested

As God would have it, I landed in the county jail at a time when a well-known evangelistic group was touring with sports stars and actors sharing personal testimonies about the life-changing power of Jesus. Oh, the power of a testimony! When they made the altar call, I gave my heart to the Lord and was prepared for whatever I might face—even what looked like five years in prison. Salvation was the first miracle I experienced in my life. I encountered the God of miracles and immediately began developing faith to believe for the working of miracles in my own life because, barring a miracle, I would be sent to prison for five years. My daughter would be without a mother after already losing her father.

Hungering and thirsting for righteousness is the foundation on which you develop faith for the working of miracles. Starting with the Book of John, I began devouring the Word. I enrolled in a correspondence Bible study program right from jail. I transferred into the Christian ward where prison ministers visited at least once and sometimes as many as three times a day for Bible studies and worship. I stayed up late at night and watched videos of preachers that some of the Christian guards brought in to edify us. I became a student of the Word—and God miraculously opened my eyes to the supernatural.

For weeks, God used passages in my paperback jailhouse Bible to highlight the significance of the number 40, which is symbolic of trials and testing. I was hardly a Bible scholar and I knew nothing about the prophetic—I was just born-again!—yet everywhere I turned in the Bible, the number 40 was illuminated. During Noah's day, it rained on the earth for 40 days and 40 nights (Genesis 7:12). Israel wandered around in the wilderness for 40 years (Numbers 32:13). Ezekiel laid on his side for 40 days as a prophetic act (Ezekiel 4:6). God was speaking to me by His Spirit and by His Word. It was as if the written Word of God jumped off the page and screamed deliverance to my soul! I just knew that I knew that I knew that I would get out of that jail on the 40th day. I had developed faith for the working of miracles in my life and it didn't take ten years, six prophecies and four angels blowing trumpets to convince me. It was putting the Word of God in my spirit that developed faith to believe for the miracle.

Confessing Deliverance From a Rhema Word

I told everyone I would be released on the 40th day—anyone who would listen. I remember telling my mother boldly that I would be released on the 40th day. She was in tears, trying to believe me. See, it was impossible for me to be released on the 40th day, naturally speaking. The judge hearing my case was scheduled for a vacation during that time period. It would be day 50 or so before I would have an opportunity to stand before him and receive my sentencing.

What's more, this is the same judge who three times denied me bond, even with an ankle bracelet on house arrest. I get it. Battery on a law enforcement office was a serious charge—and it was the officer's word against mine. But I was an upstanding member of the society for the past six and a half years. In fact, the warrant would have expired in just a few months and I would have walked away completely free if the maid hadn't called the police. Yes, I would have walked away free from criminal prosecution, but I would have remained a lost soul on my way to hell. Ephesians 1:11 is true. God really does work all things after the counsel of His will. We always have a choice to make. But He sets the stage for miracles more often than we realize. It's up to us to believe.

See, attorneys couldn't set me free. Money couldn't set me free. Not even the facts of the case could set me free. I needed a miracle—and I had faith for a miracle. I was expecting a miracle. I never considered for a moment that I wouldn't see a miracle. The difference maker was God. The God of the impossible was my witness.

"From heaven the Lord looks down and sees all mankind" (Psalm 33:13 NIV). God sees everything. God knows everything. And God turned me from a victim into a victor. I was, in fact, released on the 40th day—without ever standing before a judge. I have no criminal record. God—the God who promises all things are possible to the one who believes—vindicated me. And not only did He vindicate me—not only did He rescue me from prison—He rescued my soul from eternal hell fire. (I talk more about this experience in my books *Fervent Faith* and *Breakthrough!*)

Through that trial, I learned a lesson that has stayed with me through my Christian walk: With God all things are possible (Matthew 19:26). From a worldly perspective, I lost a lot. I lost my husband. I lost my life-savings hiring attorneys. I lost my home. I lost my job when the economy went sour during my incarceration. But I gained far more than I lost. I'm reminded of Paul the apostle's words:

> But what things were gain to me, these I have counted loss for Christ. Yet indeed I also count all things loss for the

excellence of the knowledge of Christ Jesus my Lord, for whom I have suffered the loss of all things, and count them as rubbish, that I may gain Christ and be found in Him, not having my own righteousness, which is from the law, but that which is through faith in Christ, the righteousness which is from God by faith; that I may know Him and the power of His resurrection, and the fellowship of His sufferings, being conformed to His death, if, by any means, I may attain to the resurrection from the dead.

Not that I have already attained, or am already perfected; but I press on, that I may lay hold of that for which Christ Jesus has also laid hold of me. Brethren, I do not count myself to have apprehended; but one thing I do, forgetting those things which are behind and reaching forward to those things which are ahead, I press toward the goal for the prize of the upward call of God in Christ Jesus.

Hebrews 6:4-6

I gave my heart to the Lord in 2001. When I did, I came into the Kingdom having lost most of the material wealth I had earned—and most of the relationships I had built. But I counted it all as rubbish because I had gained Christ. Not only had I gained Christ, I had encountered the God of the impossible. And that gave me an unshakeable foundation to believe Him for all things. Before too long, I would once again need to rely on that revelation.

Meditation Exercise

Do you have the revelation of Jehovah as the God of the impossible? What do you magnify when you are facing impossible situations: the miracle-working power of God or the destructive plans of the enemy? My prayer is that as you read the pages of this book, your faith will rise and you will encounter the God of the miraculous. If you set your heart now to believe the truths in this book, you will soar to new spiritual heights and overcome every enemy of your faith. It doesn't always happen overnight—or even in 40 days—but I encourage you to keep building your faith in God's Word.

2

What is a Miracle?

Miracles. We've all prayed for one. Some of us have experienced one. Others have seen one first hand. When you think of miracles, you may think of blind eyes opening or deaf ears hearing or the lame walking. Those are all indeed spectacular miracles. When you think of miracles you may also think of salvations. Indeed, being born again is the greatest miracle of all. When you think of miracles, you may even think of getting a raise right in the nick of time, avoiding a car accident by the skin of your teeth, or meeting the person of your dreams quite accidentally in a place you never go. God is always working behind the scenes and His movements to provide, protect and order our steps are often quite miraculous.

But what is a miracle, exactly? Merriam-Webster defines *miracle* as "an extraordinary event manifesting divine intervention in human affairs." And Webster's 1913 Dictionary defines miracle as "a wonder or wonderful thing" and "an event or effect contrary to the established constitution and course of things, or a deviation from the known laws of nature; a supernatural event, or one transcending the ordinary laws by which the universe is governed."

The bottom line here: A miracle is a supernatural intervention. Now that we understand the modern definitions of *miracle*, let's look at some of the original Greek in the context of miracles we read about in the Bible. *Vine's Expository Dictionary of New Testament Words* reveals that the Greek word for "miracle" is dunamis.

God's Dunamis Power

According to Vine's, *dunamis* means "power, inherent ability," and is used to describe works of a supernatural origin and character—works that could not be produced by natural agents and means. In 1 Corinthians 12:10 when Paul names the "working of miracles" as one of the gifts of the Spirit, he used the word *dunamis*. Paul also used the word *dunamis* to describe the gifts God appointed in the church: first apostles, second prophets, third teachers, after that *miracles*, then gifts of healings, helps, administrations, varieties of tongues (1 Corinthians 12:28, emphasis mine).

Some believers have the gift of working of miracles like some believers have the gift of apostle, prophet, pastor, teacher, evangelist, interpretation of tongues or administration. But every Spirit-filled believer can manifest the gifts of the Spirit as He wills. Paul told the believers at Galatia, "Therefore He who supplies the Spirit to you and works miracles among you, does He do it by the works of the law, or by the hearing of faith?"

That word "miracles" in Galatians 3:5 comes from the Greek word *dunamis*. Although the working of miracles can be a sovereign move of God, here we see that the working of miracles can be a response to our faith. We can build our faith to see the working of miracles—to see God's "power and inherent ability" manifest in our lives.

It's clear that the Holy Spirit gives some people the gift of working of miracles. These are ministers who perform miracles in the name of Jesus like a physician performs surgeries in the name of medicine. The healing evangelists of days gone by fit this bill, as do the likes of Kathryn Kuhlman and Reinhard Bonnke. We don't all walk in the gift of working of miracles like Bonnke—although God can use us to perform a miracle any time He wills—but He does give us all a measure of faith to believe in the working of miracles. We can all develop wonder-working faith to believe for God's perfect will to manifest in our lives.

Miracles: More Than Healing

The most notable miracles—and the most publicized ones—are miracles of healing. There are also stunning miracles of dying, going to heaven (or hell) and resurrecting with a story that reaches lost souls. There are miracles of instantaneous deliverances from drugs and alcohol. There are miracles of forgiveness over horrible circumstances—like the response of the Amish immediately forgiving a man who shot ten girls and killed five before committing suicide—that inspire us all to let go of our petty offenses. There are miraculous stories of divine protection and suicide prevention.

These are all wonderful miracles, but not every miracle is so dramatic that it makes newspaper headlines. We can decide to believe for the miraculous—God's supernatural intervention—in any area of our life at any time. We can believe God for miraculous provision when we have a need we can't meet. We can believe God for miracles that confuse the enemies who arise against us; miracles of supernatural strength in an emergency; miracles of supernatural peace in the midst of a storm; miracles of deliverance from danger; and even miracles of restoration and resurrection of dead things in our lives.

Need some proof? We see miracles of provision in the Bible over and over again. Jesus turned water into wine (John 2:1-11). And remember the disciples' miraculous catch of fish (Luke 5:1-11)? How about feeding the masses with a few loaves and fishes (Matthew 14:13-21)? Or the supernatural provision of tax money in the mouth of a fish (Matthew 17:24-27)? In the Old Testament, the manna from heaven was a daily miracle (Exodus 16:14-35) and let's not forget the widow's oil that never ran dry (2 Kings 4:2-7) or how 100 men were fed with 20 loaves at Gilgal (2 Kings 4:42-44).

Beyond provision, God can intervene and confuse the enemies who have risen up against you in miraculous ways. It may not be as dramatic as the plagues Moses released in Exodus 8 before the deliverance of Israel or the thunderstorm that caused panic among the Philistines in the midst of battle (1 Samuel 7:10-12). But it could be your faith-filled praise that causes your spiritual enemies to destroy one another (2 Chronicles 20:22-24) or bring the walls crumbling down that the enemy has built to keep you out of God's promises (Joshua 6:15).

If you need supernatural strength, remember Samson (Judges 14-16) or David's mighty men (1 Chronicles 11; 2 Samuel 23:8) who God anointed to do the impossible. If you need supernatural peace, remember that Jesus can calm even the most violent storms raging against you (Mark 4:35). God can miraculously deliver you from any dangerous situation just like He did for Daniel when he was in the lion's den (Daniel 6:16-23) and Shadrach, Meshach and Abednego when they were forced into the fiery furnace (Daniel 3).

If your family needs to be restored or if something dead in your life needs to be resurrected, God can work a miracle there too. Elijah raised the son of the Zarephath widow from the dead (1 Kings 17:14-16). It was no fluke. Elijah also raised the son of the Shunammite woman from the dead (2 Kings 4:32-35). In fact, Elijah's bones even revived a man from dead (2 Kings 13:21). Want some New Testament? Jesus raised the son of a Nain widow from the dead (Luke 17:11-15). Jesus also raised Jairus' daughter from the dead (Luke 8:41-55) and raised Lazarus from the dead (John 11:1-44). And, remember, Peter raised Dorcas from the dead (Acts 9:36-41) and Paul raised Eutychus from the dead (Acts 20:9-10).

If God can raise people from the dead, He can surely do a miracle in your relationships. If God can resurrect Jesus, He can surely resurrect your dead dreams. To be sure, the impossible in your life can become possible with the working of miracles. Bernard Berenson, an American historian specializing in the Renaissance, once said, "Miracles happen to those who believe in them."

Are you ready to develop faith for the working of miracles? Then get ready to put on your full armor of God because sometimes miracles happen in an instant, but most of the time you have to war for your miracle.

Meditation Exercise

People typically consider blind eyes opening—and other notable miracles—the most exciting. Most of us will never need healing from blindness or other spectacular feats. But that doesn't mean we don't need a miracle. Remember that God is the God of the miraculous and what you need concerns Him. When you've done all you can do and you are standing in faith—when you can't possibly turn a situation around on your own—you are next in line for a miracle. Like the Shirley Ceasar gospel song says, "You're next in line for a miracle. Your breakthrough. You're next in line for a miracle. You have kept the faith ... Today is your day." Expect a miracle. Sometimes it takes a while to see it. It's usually not instantaneous. But as you wait on the Lord and develop faith in His Word, you get progressively closer to the divine intervention you need.

3

The War Against Your Miracle

The enemy never wanted you to read this book. He used a series of demonic circumstances to destroy this manuscript—and almost succeeded. Clearly, seeing as you hold the book in your hands now, Christ led me into triumph as He always does (2 Corinthians 2:14). But I had to stand like Shammah (2 Samuel 23:11).

You might call it a literal war against all things possible. Yes, I triumphed. But my triumph did not come without engaging in battles, conflicts, skirmishes and feuds with the devil. For more than six months, I overcome one attack after another to preserve the truth the Holy Spirit revealed to me in this book. If I hadn't engaged in battle, I would not have won the war.

The story of how this book survived the enemy's onslaught is a strong example of the war against miraculous manifestations in your life. But it also taught me a great lesson in perseverance and standing for God's justice. The end of the story is God's vindication. Why am I telling you the end of the story before we start? Although God has already positioned you for victory in Christ, that doesn't mean you don't have to fight. Yes, the battle is the Lord's and sometimes He'll do the fighting for you. But often you have a role to play in enforcing His will in your life when the enemy comes to steal, kill and destroy. Remember Shammah. If you don't quit, you'll win.

It Started With a Revelation

I was inspired to write a book on the reality that nothing is impossible with the God of the miraculous after the Lord gave me a prophetic word about the moving of His Spirit—and why we see so little of it. I shared that story in the introduction of this book and won't rehash it here. Suffice it to say that I was convinced the Body of Christ needed a greater revelation of the "God of all things possible" in order to stir faith that would meet the anointing and manifest the miraculous. So I diligently studied the topic of "all things possible" and preached a two-part series on the topic. I had so much marvelous truth on it that I began writing a book.

I was 80 percent done with the manuscript and had set it aside to "let it breathe" as writers often do. Suddenly, my two-year-old computer completely died.

Computer hard drives should last three to five years—and I've had them last much, much longer than that. But my hard drive was dead. And my manuscript was on it. I had most of my hard drive backed up but had forgotten to back up the manuscript. The enemy pounced on my mistake. I believed God for a miraculous hard drive recovery but the computer remained in its grave.

I carried the beast of a machine to the computer store, but the technician could not retrieve my files. He removed the hard drive and I sent it to a highly recommended data recovery service whose advertisements guaranteed they could retrieve 99.999 percent of the files on any damaged hard drive within 10 days. This firm worked for major Fortune 500 companies and was reputable on all fronts. My cost: $1,200. Well, I had spent more than 100 hours studying and writing this manuscript and I knew there was revelation in the text that would be lost if I could not retrieve the file. So I shelled out the $1,200 and waited patiently for about 45 days for the materials that had been promised to me within 10 days.

Side Skirmishes in the Midst of War

In the meantime, I bought a new computer and started trying to recreate what I could. That's when I found myself in a separate battle designed to discourage me. After I got everything set up on the brand new machine—about 20 hours of software installation and configuration—the hard drive failed. The computer was right out of the box! Yet the hard drive failed.

The technicians said it was a fluke. I actually had to battle with the retailer to get my money back. They wanted me to send it out for repair even though I purchased it just 48 hours earlier. I called the manufacturer who interceded for me. The retailer returned my money and I set out to buy a new computer directly from the manufacturer and go through the 20-hour installation process once again.

As another side battle to frustrate me, when I left the store and went to enter my car I noticed a huge dent in the front panel. Someone in the parking lot had crushed the front of my brand new vehicle and fled the scene. The insurance company deductible for having it repaired was $500.

Weeks later, I was still waiting for my far overdue hard drive recovery. I continued pressing them and got nothing but excuses until they finally called me with "great news." They assured me they had my book files. They told me they were actually reading the material and everything was intact. I asked them several times to make completely sure, since the only thing on the hard drive that I needed—and that wasn't backed up—was this manuscript and related materials. They once again guaranteed me this file was readable and charged me the $1,200.

I was so relieved. I was praising God ... until I received the recovered hard drive files. The employee at the hardware recovery service lied to me. The file was corrupted and I could not open it. When I called to ask them what was going on, they claimed they never guaranteed the file would open and that they had never suggested it was working on their end before they sent it to me. Boldfaced lies!

The Real War Begins

I was shocked that what was supposed to be a reputable company would lie to this extreme. I contacted the owner and explained the situation. He stood by his employees and refused to review the case further. I did everything under the sun to try to open the corrupted file. I put it through file crackers and converters and various software programs. I literally spent 10 hours in desperation trying to make it work. Finally, I called another hardware recovery service and told them what happened. They offered to look at the hard drive and try to retrieve the file. They assured me they would not charge me a penny if they could not get the manuscript. I took a chance. And, thank God, they were able to retrieve the file. Of course, I had to pay them $1,000 for their service.

With the file in hand and a statement from the successful file retrieval company, I went back to the first vendor—the vendor who lied about retrieving the file—and asked them to refund my money. They refused. I told them I would dispute it with my credit card company. The owner told me he had plenty of people try to dispute charges with their credit card company in the past and no one had ever been successful. I declared to him that I would be the first. He didn't flinch.

Unfortunately, my credit card company told me it had been too long since the initial charge for them to dispute it. At first, my heart sunk. But they asked me to send them the information anyway. When they saw the nasty e-mails from the vendor and his bold claims that no customer had ever won a credit card dispute against him, my representative waxed bold and said he would see what he could do to right this wrong. I told God right then and there that if I got the money back I would donate it to my church. I wasn't interested in the money. I was interested in justice. This dishonest vendor needed to see that he could not continue to rip people off and get away with it.

Vengeance is God's

Within 45 days, I had a check from my credit card company in the amount that the dishonest vendor had charged me. I was thrilled. I thanked God, wrote out a check to my church for the same amount, and saved the letter from the credit card company as a testimony to God's faithfulness. It was a miracle.

Yes, God vindicated me. I had to keep my heart right through the process. I had to take a Luke 18 approach and continue day and night to insist on what belonged to me in prayer. I had to persevere the side attacks from the enemy—like the broken computer and the dented new car. I had to take natural courses to find a new solution to my corrupted manuscript problem. I had to approach the credit card company with the story.

The point is, God vindicated me but I had to do things in the natural to pave the way for Him to work. I wasn't likely to recover my manuscript or my money if I had prayed only and without taking action. Faith without works is dead. Yes, sometimes God will move miraculously without our lifting a finger. He could have caused that corrupted file to open on my desktop. Surely, He could have. Remember, I asked Him for a miracle before I went to all the trouble to go to another vendor and dispute the credit card charge. But He chose to let me battle for my miracle rather than giving me instant gratification. I don't understand all the reasons why, but I know that the experience made me stronger—and it taught the dishonest vendor a lesson. Maybe he won't be so quick to rip people off in the future. If what I went through saved others some trouble, so be it. I'm wiser and stronger now.

Why We Have to Take Authority

Christ has all authority. He spoiled the principalities and powers and made a show of them openly, triumphing over them in it (Colossians 2:15). Of course, when you read that passage of Scripture, the Bible doesn't say, "Therefore, let no one tell you that you need to take authority over the devil." No, verse 16 of the Second Chapter of Colossians says, "Therefore let no man judge you in meat, or in drink, or in respect of an holyday, or of the new moon, or of the Sabbath days…"

I can't tell you how many times people have told me that we don't need to take authority over the devil because Jesus already finished the work. Christ finished the work of the Lamb of God that takes away the sin of the world, yes. Christ has the keys to death and hell (Revelation 1:8). But I submit to you that if it were no longer necessary to take authority over the works of darkness from which we've been translated, the apostles Paul, Peter and James wouldn't have signaled the need for spiritual warfare.

Paul told us succinctly that "we wrestle not against flesh and blood, but against principalities, against powers, against the rulers of the darkness of this world, against spiritual wickedness in high places" (Ephesians 6:12) Why does Paul paint such a descriptive picture and offer a hierarchy of demonic forces we have to wrestle if we didn't have a role to play in spiritual warfare?

Paul also mentions the weapons of our warfare, which are not carnal, but mighty through God to the pulling down of strong holds (2 Corinthians 10:4). Why would we need weapons if we weren't in a spiritual war against a spiritual enemy?

Paul tells his spiritual son Timothy to be a good soldier (2 Timothy 2:3) and to war a good warfare (1 Timothy 1:18). Why would he give that advice if Timothy wasn't in a war with an unseen enemy? Paul also told us not to give place to the devil (Ephesians 4:27) and warned about the snare of the devil (1 Timothy 3:7; 2 Timothy 2:26). Why would he offer these admonitions if they weren't warranted? The enemy is real and he wants to rob your miracle from you. You are indeed in a war.

Then, we have James, who told us to resist the devil and he will flee (James 4:7). And Peter, who warned us to be sober and vigilant, because our adversary the devil, as a roaring lion, walketh about seeking whom he may devour (1 Peter 5:8-9 KJV). Peter told us to resist him, standing firm in the faith. Of course, Paul also told us to fight the good fight of faith (1 Timothy 6:12). Should we ignore all these warnings and instructions? God forbid.

All of these Scriptures suggest that the devil is still wreaking havoc on the earth. Havoc on the earth—sickness, disease, murders, immorality and the like—is not God's will. Jesus spoiled the principalities and powers. But the word "spoiled" doesn't mean neutered and made powerless. Jesus plundered the kingdom of darkness. The kingdom of darkness and all the principalities and powers that call it home, lost authority over the born-again believer. But we still have to enforce the Kingdom rule of law on earth.

To say that Jesus spoiling the principalities and powers means those principalities and powers cannot attempt to stand in the way of our miracle is like saying a thief can't break into your house because there's a law against it. The devil doesn't follow the rules. He's been a sinner from the beginning (1 John 3:8).

The Believer's Authority

God loves us with an undying love. David marveled over this in the eighth Psalm. When he considered the work of God's fingers, the moon and the stars, which He set in place, David wondered why God is mindful of mere mortals. But God is not only mindful of us, He's given us exceeding great and precious promises. Let's read this prophetic psalm:

Yet you made them only a little lower than God and crowned them with glory and honor. You gave them charge of everything you made, putting all things under their authority—the flocks and the herds and all the wild animals, the birds in the sky, the fish in the sea, and everything that swims the ocean currents. O Lord, our Lord, your majestic name fills the earth!

Psalm 8:5-9 (NLT)

David was referring to what we would call the old covenant. We have a better covenant in Christ, which we will discuss in a later chapter. Part of that covenant is a right to exercise the authority of Christ. Jesus gave us His authority—and He expects us to use it to enforce His rule of law. When we do, we're also making a way for miracles in our lives because the devil actively works to hinder the manifestation of your healing, your deliverance, your breakthrough, and your covenant blessings.

Remember, we are seated with Christ in heavenly places (Ephesians 2:6). And we are joint-heirs with Christ (Romans 8:17). We reign as kings in life by Christ Jesus (Romans 5:17). Jesus gave us the keys of the Kingdom of heaven (Matthew 16:19). Whatsoever we bind on earth shall be bound in heaven, and whatsoever we loose on earth shall be loosed in heaven. That's authority. Can you see it?

Let's look at some Scriptural witnesses dealing with our Christ-given authority, which is backed up by God Himself.

> Then He called His twelve disciples together and gave them power and authority over all demons, and to cure diseases. He sent them to preach the kingdom of God and to heal the sick. And He said to them, "Take nothing for the journey, neither staffs nor bag nor bread nor money; and do not have two tunics apiece."
>
> Luke 9:1-3

Jesus gave us authority over all devils—not just some of them. And He expects us to use that authority to help make all things possible to those who believe. The anointing is looking for faith. Where the two meet, you find miracles. I love the Amplified translation of Luke 10:19.

> Behold! I have given you authority and power to trample upon serpents and scorpions, and [physical and mental strength and ability] over all the power

that the enemy [possesses]; and nothing shall in any way harm you.

Luke 10:19 (AMP)

Again, we see that Jesus gave us authority and power over all the power of the devil. There isn't one special secret power the devil can use that can stand against the authority Christ delegated to us. There is no spiritual kryptonite, so to speak, that will bring us down. As long as we remain in Him, walking in Him, clothed in Him and exercising our delegated authority, the devil can by no means harm us. Listen to what else Jesus said about our delegated authority:

Jesus approached and, breaking the silence, said to them, "All authority (all power of rule) in heaven and on earth has been given to Me. Go then and make disciples of all the nations, baptizing them into the name of the Father and of the Son and of the Holy Spirit..."

Matthew 28:18-19 (AMP)

Jesus has all authority in heaven and on earth. God gave it to Him and He gave it to us. We need this authority to help others see the miraculous manifest in their lives. Helping people realize all things possible begins with witnessing, making disciples and baptizing people with the Holy Spirit.

Increasing Your Authority

Our spiritual authority can also increase. Do you remember the parable of the 10 servants? A nobleman went away to a distant empire to be crowned king and return. Before he left, he called together 10 of his servants, gave them each one pound of silver and said, "Occupy till I come." The servants had plenty of opposition from haters who refused to respect the nobleman or to be ruled over by him.

After the nobleman was crowned king, he returned and called in the servants to whom he had given the money. He wanted to find out what the profits were. The first servant made 10 times as much as he was entrusted with. The nobleman's response: "Well done, thou good servant: because thou hast been faithful in a very little, thou have authority over ten cities" (Luke 19:17 KJV).

You know the story. The next servant gained five pounds of silver, and the next hid his in a napkin, making the nobleman angry. The nobleman called him a wicked servant and confiscated the money. Let's listen in:

> Then, turning to the others standing nearby, the king ordered, 'Take the money from this servant, and give it to the one who has ten pounds.'

"'But, master,' they said, 'he already has ten pounds!'

"'Yes,' the king replied, 'and to those who use well what they are given, even more will be given. But from those who do nothing, even what little they have will be taken away.'"

Luke 19:24-26 (NLT)

Christ gave us authority. God gave us the measure of faith. When we exercise our Christ-given authority with our God-given faith, the Holy Ghost shows up on the scene to make all things possible to him who believes. God expects us to exercise our authority in Christ to be fruitful, multiply, take dominion, heal the sick, cleanse the lepers, cast out demons, preach the Gospel and everything else Christ did while He walked the earth. We cannot tap into the fullness of our all things possible covenant—we can't enforce God's will on the earth—if we don't exercise our authority in Christ.

Meditation Exercise

Are there areas of your life where you've handed your authority over the enemy? We can't take authority over the devil when we're acting like the devil. In other words, Christ gave us authority but if we aren't using it—or if we are cooperating with the enemy in any area of our life, knowingly or unknowingly—then we are not going to be successful in waging war over the devil.

If you aren't seeing all things possible in your life, consider whether you are using your authority or if you are forfeiting your authority by consistently practicing sin and breaking fellowship with the One who gives you authority. If you aren't missing it in either area, then keep taking authority. The enemy doesn't always flee the first time you resist him. He tries to wear out the saints (Daniel 7:25) with an onslaught of attacks. But if you keep standing in your place of authority, you will outlast the devil and see all things possible.

www.jenniferleclaire.org

4

Warring for Your Miracle

You'll probably never be abandoned with a baby. You'll probably never land in jail for a crime you didn't commit. You'll probably never lose every penny you have. And you probably won't see a book manuscript held hostage on a corrupted hard drive. But you will go through trials and you may need a miracle to get through to the other side. I'm not prophesying doom and gloom over you. Jesus said, "In the world you will have tribulation; but be of good cheer, I have overcome the world" (John 16:33).

I've learned that trials are relative. In other words, you don't need to have a Job-like trial to feel like your world is falling apart. I've been through trials large and small—and I'm sure you have too. One of the keys to getting through the storm—no matter how much devastation that storm brings in its path—is to understand that all things are possible to him who believes (Mark 9:23) and then understand what *all things* really means. Armed with this revelation, you are ready to wage war for your miracle, whether that's provision, deliverance, healing or something else only God can do.

The concept of "all things" runs throughout the entire Bible from cover to cover. In fact, the King James Bible speaks of "all things" 201 times. But did Jesus really mean "all things are possible to him who believes?" (Mark 9:23) And, if so, what does "all things" really mean?

Of course, Jesus meant what He said. When God speaks, truth is established and once that truth is established nothing can change it. God does not have a loose tongue and He doesn't make promises He can't keep. We may go back on our Word, but God doesn't go back on His Word.

We need to settle this "all things" question in our hearts once and for all because sometimes you can't find a specific promise in Scripture to stand on. Oh, the Scripture may be there but you may be too overwhelmed to find it or you may not have enough knowledge of the Word to know what belongs to you.

Building Faith to Fight for Your Miracle

The Bible makes us more than 7,000 promises. Some are conditional. Some are unconditional. But each and every one is available as a benefit of our covenant. (We'll look more at our covenant in a later chapter.) God has given us His Word and He is not a man that He should lie (Numbers 23:19). Yet, sometimes in the midst of the pressures of every day life—and in the heat of the battle raging in our minds—our emotions cloud our view. Instead of meditating on God's promise for our current situation—whether its healing, finances, peace, wisdom, protection, etc.—we meditate on our raging circumstances and remember our past failures. But if you can just remember two simple words, you can reconnect with the hope that anchors your soul long enough to find the appropriate promise on which to stand. Those two words are "all things." Your miracle is included under the all things banner.

Let me put it another way. How can you fight for something if you don't know it belongs to you? When you take ownership of God's promises—when you get the revelation that God's promises belong to you— you'll fight the good fight of faith to see them manifest in your life little by little. You may already be a student of the Word. You may already accurately wield the Sword of the Spirit when the enemy comes to kill, steal and destroy the seeds—or the impending harvest—of God's promises in your life. But if you aren't seeing God's promises manifest spiritually, mentally, socially, emotionally, financially, and physically—if you are walking in continual defeat in some area of your life—then it could be possible that you are missing an arrow in your quiver.

Again, that arrow is the revelation of two words that are repeated over and over again in the Word of God: "all things." There is miracle-working power in believing those two little words. Believing all things are possible will not only stabilize your soul during the downpours, hurricanes, tempests, tornadoes and various other storms, it will also strengthen your heart to go through the test and trial with godly character. If you are ignorant to what "all things" really means, then you are missing a faith-builder that can take you through even the Job-like trials.

What Does "All Things" Mean?

It's been said that a man who believes that all things are possible approaches the unconventional with an open mind and a fearless heart. An open mind and a fearless heart set the stage for miracles.

So, then, what does "all things" mean in Scripture? Well, I don't know about you, but I'm the kind of believer who believes God literally. I don't try to figure out what He meant. He meant what He said. When He says something in His Word, I take it at face value. So when God says "all" He means "all." He doesn't mean some, much or most. He means all. One dictionary definition for "all" is "as much as possible." So you might say, as much as possible is possible if you believe. And we know that with God all things are possible (Matthew 19:26). With pure faith, nothing will be impossible to you (Matthew 17:20).

Matthew 17:20 carries an important point: Accessing all things possible requires faith. You have to develop faith to see the working of miracles in your life. Just so there's no way for the devil to talk you out of the truth that's in the rest of this book, let's go ahead and dissect the word "all" once and for all and reinforce your faith for all things possible to him who believes (Mark 9:23). Begin building your faith for miracles even now!

The New Testament word for "all" in Scriptures that reference "all things" comes from the Greek word "pas." Guess what it means? There aren't six or seven definitions. It's very clear. "Pas" means "all." So what does "all" mean? "All" means the "whole amount, quantity or extent of." All things means everything. Nothing is excluded in all things. All things includes all that exists. In fact, "all" means more than that. Because if God doesn't already have what you need, the Creator of heaven and earth can make it for you.

Creative Miracles Still Happen!

Meditate on that for a minute. It's a powerful faith builder for the miraculous—and it's totally Scriptural. The creation of the universe was a creative miracle. The creation of man was a creative miracle. The manna sent from heaven to feed the Israelites was a creative miracle (Exodus 16:14-35). The water from the rock was a creative miracle (Exodus 17:5-7). The multiplication of the widow's oil was a creative miracle (2 Kings 4:2-7). The man whose withered hand was restored was a creative miracle (Matthew 12:10).

Twice Jesus fed thousands when there was only enough food available to feed a few. In Matthew 14, Jesus used five loaves and two fish to feed 5,000 men (not counting women and children) and in Matthew 15 He used a boy's lunch to feed 4,000 men (not counting women and children). Naturally speaking, there wasn't enough food to go around. So the Creator of heaven and earth made it for them.

Is your faith for creative miracles rising? Yes, you say, but that's just Bible stuff. Well, I'm here to tell you that God is still performing creative miracles today. Operation Mobilization, an international missions ministry, tells the story of God miraculously creating food at a prison outreach in Mexico.

According to a report in *Charisma News*, the outreach began with songs of praise and worship. A former drug addict gave his testimony. The Word of God was preached and many came to Christ. When the service concluded, it was time to distribute the food. They only had enough food for 70 inmates: "We prayed for God to multiply the food," says Tami. "By the end of the service there were 200 men attending." Their prayer was answered. "I could hardly believe it, but it happened. As we were handing the food out to the inmates, it didn't run out. We even had enough plates and spoons for 200 men!"

We know that God is not limited by what exists. He is the Creator of all things. If something needs to be created, He has the power to do it—and He wants to do it for you. How can I say that? I can say that because I read John 14:13 through the lens of the original Greek. Jesus said, "And whatsoever ye shall ask in my name, that will I do, that the Father may be glorified in the Son."

That's quite a promise in itself. But when you dig out the Greek meaning you get an even richer promise. The translators used the words "shall" and "will" because these are the strongest assertions one can make in the English language. But the verse literally means something much stronger. It means, "If you will ask anything in My Name, if I don't have it, I'll make it for you."

Now, let me balance that out. If you ask with the wrong motives, forget it. James warns, "You ask and do not receive, because you ask amiss, that you may spend it on your pleasures" (James 4:3). If you are asking for a big house because you lust after the admiration of men, you are abusing this principle and are in danger of tapping into New Age secrets. Don't go there. When I'm talking about creative miracles, I'm talking about things in line with God's will. I am not endorsing the prosperity gospel, though I do believe in prosperity. I am not endorsing name-it-claim-it, blab-it-grab-it, watered down and hyped up gospels.

But all that controversy has, to some extent, robbed genuine believers of the determination to press in for God's perfect will. People stop praying for their lost family members because they think the case is too hard for God. No! Believe for a miracle! People give up the battle against cancer because of the doctor's report. No! Believe for a miracle. Sometimes people die in a lost condition. Sometimes people die from cancer. Sometimes you lose your house or your spouse. Despite the fact that no one has a smooth ride in every area of their life all the time, we should still believe that God will work all things together for good to those that love Him and are called according to His purpose (Romans 8:28). Indeed, there's a miracle in that verse! Sometimes we end up in impossible situations. That's why you need to build your faith for all things possible.

Overcoming the 'Show Me' Faith

Oral Roberts, a healing evangelist that has gone home to be with the Lord, believed for creative miracles and saw them. But that doesn't mean he didn't struggle to believe. If you are struggling to believe for a creative miracle, listen to his testimony. Roberts once spoke on television about his reaction to a mother bringing a little boy into a crusade who had been born without a hip socket. Roberts said:

"That was the time I learned there are different stages of faith—certainly different stages of faith in my prayers. And when she said that her little boy had been born without a hip socket, and she wanted me to pray I said, 'Well, I can't do that.' Now, there was a huge crowd out in front of me witnessing the scene. And I said, 'I believe this would take a creative miracle and in the resurrection of his body from the dead God will give him a new hip socket. But I don't have the faith for that.'

And she said, 'Oral Roberts, I don't ask you to have the faith. You pray and I'll do the believing.' Well, the whole crowd just gushed out. I could tell they were with her. I prayed my little two-cent prayer and he hobbled off on his crutches and I said to myself, 'Just like I thought, God is not going to do that in this world.' So the next night when they drove me to the tent and I got out there was a man that said, 'Remember the little boy without the hip socket?' I said, 'Yes.' He said, 'That's him running and jumping on the platform.'

I said, 'You shouldn't have someone up there doing that unless there's proof of the healing.' He said, 'Brother Roberts, the little boy has been back to his doctor. He's got a new hip socket.' I said, 'Wait a minute. Let me get up there.' Well, I got up on the platform and I put my hand on his hip and remembered there was a sunk in place. I could put my hand virtually into it. And I put my hand on it and it was filled.

I said to this woman, 'What happened?' And she said, 'I took him back to the same doctor that delivered him and he's pronounced him with a new hip socket.' Well, then of course I began to rejoice and praise the Lord and immediately I went into a different stage of faith. In those days there were not that many healings going on in the world in a big public sense before a great crowd, before television. We were breaking new ground all the time."

See, Roberts had never seen it done so he couldn't believe for it. But he learned a lesson: It doesn't matter if you've ever seen it done. It doesn't matter if nobody else has ever received the miracle you are believing God for. If it's according to God's Word—if you can find a Scripture to cover it—it's possible. And here's a Scripture that covers it all: All things are possible to him who believes (Mark 9:23).

Unbelief: The Root of the Impossible

Are you ready to break new ground in your faith? You've probably heard it said, "If God ever did it for anybody, He'll do it for you." Don't limit God like that. Even if God has never done it for anybody, He can do it for you!

Again, all things are possible to him who believes (Mark 9:23). Does that mean there are no impossibilities in the things of God? Nothing is too hard for God (Genesis 18:14), but there are impossibilities in the realm of the spirit. For example, it is impossible for God to lie (Hebrews 6:18). When God speaks, truth is established. It is also impossible for the blood of bulls and goats to take away sins (Hebrews 10:3). That's why God sent His only begotten Son into the world, to sacrifice His sinless self for the sin of the world.

Let's look at a few of the places where the Bible talks about what's impossible for you and me. As we do, you'll notice the root of that impossibility: unbelief. Indeed, you'll see with your own eyes that when the Bible talks about what's impossible the picture is typically fairly grim.

> For it is impossible for those who were once enlightened, and have tasted the heavenly gift, and have become partakers of the Holy Spirit, and have tasted the good word of God and the powers of the age to come, if they fall away, to renew them again to repentance, since they crucify again for themselves the Son of God, and put Him to an open shame.
>
> Hebrews 6:4-6

> But without faith it is impossible to please Him, for he who comes to God must believe that He is, and that He is a rewarder of those who diligently seek Him.
>
> Hebrews 11:6

Can you see it? The opposite of faith is unbelief. Unbelief effectively ties God's hands from manifesting the miraculous. We know that Jesus could not do many mighty works in Nazareth because of the unbelief among the people there (Mark 6:5). Notice that Mark didn't say Jesus chose not to do mighty works. The Bible says Jesus *could not* do many mighty works. He could not do the miracles He did in other places. Just as faith receives all things possible, unbelief blocks miracles God wants to see manifest in your life. Resolve in your heart right now to begin to believe for all things possible in your life and look for the little foxes of unbelief that are spoiling your faith vine.

Here's one final contrast between the impossible and the possible in the Kingdom: Jesus said it's impossible for a rich man to enter the Kingdom of God—but with God all things are possible (Matthew 19:23-26). That shows you the limitations of humans and the omnipotence of our miracle-working God in one breath. And again, Jesus said with God nothing shall be impossible (Luke 1:37). And the things that are impossible in your own strength are possible with God (Luke 18:27). There are things we can do with the God-given life, talents and abilities within us. But there are things that are impossible without God's intervention. Those things are called miracles. The good news is Jesus said, "If thou canst believe, all things are possible to him that believeth" (Mark 9:23 KJV).

With Signs Following

It's not all about you. Unbelief can also affect your ability to minister the supernatural to others. Remember the man with the lunatic son? The Bible says he was sore vexed. Quite often the demons threw him into the fire and other times threw him into the river. Those demons were trying to kill him! The boy's father brought him to Jesus' disciples and they could not cure him. Jesus was disappointed when the man told them that His disciples, who had been given authority to cast out devils in His name, could not get the job done. Then He reveals why:

> Then Jesus answered and said, "O faithless and perverse generation, how long shall I be with you? How long shall I bear with you? Bring him here to Me." And Jesus rebuked the demon, and it came out of him; and the child was cured from that very hour.
>
> Then the disciples came to Jesus privately and said, "Why could we not cast it out?"
>
> So Jesus said to them, "Because of your unbelief; for assuredly, I say to you, if you have faith as a mustard seed, you will say to this mountain, 'Move from here to there,' and it will move; and nothing will be impossible for you.
>
> Matthew 17:17-20

Sometimes unbelief that blocks the working of miracles stems from not knowing what the truth is. That was probably the case before you came to Christ. You didn't have faith to believe in Jesus as Savior because you had never heard the gospel—or you never really paid close attention to what you were hearing and weighed it in your heart. It doesn't take mountain-sized faith to move a mountain. It just takes a spec of pure faith to get the job done. You can read more about battling doubt and unbelief in my book *Faith Magnified*. In the next chapter, we'll build up our faith in our all things covenant with God so we won't fall for the devil's lies anymore. Get ready to see your miracle!

Meditation Exercise

There are people who need a touch from God all over the world—and all around you. They need to know that all things are possible. But we must believe the Word in our own hearts if we are going to minister to others in power. Miraculous signs—casting out demons, speaking new languages, immunity from deadly things, and healing the sick—follow believers (Mark 16:17-18). But we must believe it first. We believe it, then we see it. If we saw it first, we wouldn't have to walk by faith. Seeing by faith is believing. What are you believing God for? Find a Scripture that applies to your situation and meditate on it every day for 15 minutes.

5

A Miraculous Covenant

When I began to study the use of the phrase "all things" in God's Word, I was amazed at the depth of what it includes. Starting from Genesis and right on through to Revelation, "all things" includes everything you will ever need for your spirit, soul or body.

When God created Adam, He gave him dominion over all things. All things included the fish of the sea, the fowl of the air, the cattle and all the earth and every creeping thing that creeps on the earth (Genesis 1:26).

> Then God blessed them, and God said to them, "Be fruitful and multiply; fill the earth and subdue it; have dominion over the fish of the sea, over the birds of the air, and over every living thing that moves on the earth"
>
> Genesis 1:28

Indeed, God gave Adam "all things"—except permission to eat from the Tree of the Knowledge of Good and Evil. We know that Adam committed high treason by willfully disobeying God's command and following Eve into sin and spiritual death. Adam lost his dominion authority over all things, but God's plan for His creation didn't change.

Noah marks a new beginning. After the flood, God made an all things possible covenant with Noah and his sons that sounds strikingly familiar to what He said to Adam years earlier:

> "So God blessed Noah and his sons, and said to them: "Be fruitful and multiply, and fill the earth. And the fear of you and the dread of you shall be on every beast of the earth, on every bird of the air, on all that move on the earth, and on

all the fish of the sea. They are given into your hand. Every moving thing that lives shall be food for you. I have given you all things, even as the green herbs. But you shall not eat flesh with its life, that is, its blood.

Genesis 9:1-4

God's covenant people once again had dominion over all things. Of course, the key word is "covenant." The "all things" promise belongs to those who are in covenant with God. Once reserved for Hebrews, Jesus Christ made the all things covenant possible for the Gentiles. It's a covenant that is activated through the miracle of salvation. That makes it a miraculous covenant. We are justified by faith, not by works of the Law (Galatians 2:16; Romans 3:28). And if anyone is in Christ, he is a new creation; old things have passed away; behold, all things have become new (2 Corinthians 5:17). When all things became new all things became possible.

And here's something even better: Although it's a new covenant, it doesn't nullify the promises God made to His covenant people throughout biblical history. Long before Moses miraculously received the 10 commandments and various other laws, Abraham made a covenant with God that becomes part of our all things possible promise.

Fast forward a few thousand years after God encountered Noah and we see Abraham, who was an old man. The Bible says the Lord had blessed

Abraham in all things (Genesis 24:1). Abraham was the tenth generation from Noah and the 20th generation from Adam. What did all things mean in his life? Well, let's explore this for a moment.

The Abrahamic Covenant

God made 60 promises to Abraham. Taken together, the Abrahamic covenant guaranteed blessings like physical health and material prosperity. The promise of healing and prosperity wasn't just for Abraham's birthline, though. It was for Abraham's seed. That includes us. Consider the Apostle Paul's theology on the matter:

> Just as Abraham "believed God, and it was accounted to him for righteousness." Therefore know that only those who are of faith are sons of Abraham. And the Scripture, foreseeing that God would justify the Gentiles by faith, preached the gospel to Abraham beforehand, saying, "In you all the nations shall be blessed." So then those who are of faith are blessed with believing Abraham.

> For as many as are of the works of the law are under the curse; for it is written, "Cursed is everyone who does not continue in all things which are written in the book of the law, to do them." But that no one is justified by the law in the

sight of God is evident, for "the just shall live by faith." Yet the law is not of faith, but "the man who does them shall live by them."

Christ has redeemed us from the curse of the law, having become a curse for us (for it is written, "Cursed is everyone who hangs on a tree"), that the blessing of Abraham might come upon the Gentiles in Christ Jesus, that we might receive the promise of the Spirit through faith.

Galatians 3:6-14

Now, Hebrews 8:6 says Jesus "has obtained a more excellent ministry, inasmuch as He is also Mediator of a better covenant, which was established on better promises." We get the promises of the New Covenant and the promises of the Old Covenant. So in order to further understand what our all things covenant includes, we need to go all the way back to Deuteronomy 28, which talks about the blessings for obedience and the curses for disobedience. Christ redeemed us from the curse of the law. That leaves all things in the blessing for obedience available to us. And there are miracles in the mix! These miracles are possible for those who believe.

Of course, we have to walk circumspectly with the Lord. He won't break covenant with us, but too often His children break fellowship with Him. You can't practice sin and walk in the covenant promises at the same time. So if you aren't right with God, take some time to truly repent—stop sinning! Cry out to God to help you overcome the sin and believe for His sufficient grace to strengthen you against it.

Will You Believe the Blessing?

You've probably read it before, but let's review what belongs to us and what we're redeemed from. Looking at both sides of the blessing-curse coin sheds a little more light on all things possible. I want to look at this in the Message translation in hope that the plain language will make this point plain.

> "Now it shall come to pass, if you diligently obey the voice of the Lord your God, to observe carefully all His commandments which I command you today, that the Lord your God will set you high above all nations of the earth. And all these blessings shall come upon you and overtake you, because you obey the voice of the Lord your God:
>
> "Blessed shall you be in the city, and blessed shall you be in the country.
>
> "Blessed shall be the fruit of your body, the produce of your ground and the increase of your herds, the increase of your cattle and the offspring of your flocks.

"Blessed shall be your basket and your kneading bowl.

"Blessed shall you be when you come in, and blessed shall you be when you go out.

Deuteronomy 28:1-6 (The Message)

Let's pause right here for a minute. All of these blessings come raining down because you have responded to the voice of your God. In other words, these blessings belong to you because you responded to God's call of salvation. The Holy Spirit convicted your heart and you obeyed His leading into the mercies of God. Now, you are a new creature in Christ, a covenant believer who can continue responding to the voice of the Lord through the written Word and the still small voice of the Holy Spirit. Let's continue to see what all things possible includes. I like how The Message Bible makes it so plain:

God's blessing inside the city, God's blessing in the country; God's blessing on your children, the crops of your land, the young of your livestock, the calves of your herds, the lambs of your flocks. God's blessing on your basket and bread bowl; God's blessing in

your coming in, God's blessing in your
going out.

Deuteronomy 28:3-6 (The Message)

Guaranteed Victory in Battle

Do you have your shoutin' clothes on? Everywhere
you go, everything you own and everything you do is
blessed. In other words, all things—you, your kids,
your possessions—all things in your domain are
blessed. So if anything in your life doesn't look like
this passage of Scripture—if it doesn't look like it has
God's blessing all over it—you need to extend your
faith for all things. And, again, if you are practicing
sin you need to repent and let God restore your life.
Let's continue with the next verses:

> The Lord will cause your enemies who
> rise against you to be defeated before
> your face; they shall come out against
> you one way and flee before you seven
> ways.
> Deuteronomy 28:7

I'm sorry. I have to stop right here for just a moment
and rejoice. If the enemy has ever attacked you and
you didn't know what to do, you'll understand. Our
all things covenant includes divine protection. Yes,
we need to be prepared to run to the battle line, but

when we do our part—whatever God says our part is—He will do His part. He will defeat our enemies, not by might, not by power but by His Spirit (Zechariah 4:6)

"We do not wrestle against flesh and blood, but against principalities, against powers, against the rulers of the darkness of this age, against spiritual hosts of wickedness in the heavenly places" (Ephesians 6:12). But you have the whole armor of God so that you are able to withstand in the evil day, and having done all, to stand. Glory!

I've met with enemies natural and spiritual—though I have come to understand that the natural enemies are motivated by the demonic forces Paul lists in Ephesians 6. When you are in the midst of spiritual warfare, you can get over the top more quickly if you'll remember the Deuteronomy 28:7 part of your all things covenant with God—the Lord will cause your enemies who rise against you to be defeated before your face; they shall come out against you one way and flee before you seven ways. When the enemy attacks you, confess that verse out of your mouth with confidence.

Spiritual battles tend to come at me in clusters. Maybe you can relate. One time, my mother underwent heart surgery only to find out that the doctors could not fix the problem. According to the surgeon, she could throw a blood clot and have a massive stroke at any time. That kind of news intends to breed fear in your heart.

The next day, my then-15-year-old daughter was left stranded in an international airport after a missions group failed to arrive on time to pick her up.

Again, the spirit of fear launched a fiery dart. That same group neglected to collect the proper travel documents to give her entry into the foreign country to which they were traveling.

The next day, a colleague I recommended for a preaching engagement failed to show up and later attacked me when I suggested he needed to repent. I lost my rental car keys. I hit my head so hard I was too dizzy to drive. All the while I was living on virtually no sleep in a city 700 miles away from home, trying to seek God for the next chapter in my life.

When it seems like all hell is breaking lose against us, we have to go back to the Word—even if we have to get a concordance and look for Scriptures that may relate to our specific trial—and find out what God has to say about the situation. But if you are in such a battle that you can't even manage to think straight, you can rely on this one verse as part of your all things possible covenant: "The Lord will cause your enemies who rise against you to be defeated before your face; they shall come out against you one way and flee before you seven ways" (Deuteronomy 28:7). Take some time to write down a few of these key verses so that when you are in the heat of the battle you can draw them out—and speak them out.

Prosperity Promises
Our all things possible covenant with God includes victory in warfare. And it's very possible and most likely probable that you will have to fight the good fight of faith to receive God's best for your life in

every area. One thing you'll have to fight for—even if it means fighting against your own wrong mindsets about God—is prosperity. God's all things possible covers it, but the enemy doesn't want you to have it.

> And the Lord will grant you plenty of goods, in the fruit of your body, in the increase of your livestock, and in the produce of your ground, in the land of which the Lord swore to your fathers to give you. The Lord will open to you His good treasure, the heavens, to give the rain to your land in its season, and to bless all the work of your hand. You shall lend to many nations, but you shall not borrow. And the Lord will make you the head and not the tail; you shall be above only, and not be beneath, if you heed the commandments of the Lord your God, which I command you today, and are careful to observe them. So you shall not turn aside from any of the words which I command you this day, to the right or the left, to go after other gods to serve them.
>
> Deuteronomy 28:11-14

You have two parts to play in the all things covenant—believe it and obey the voice of God. Of course, we'll never be perfect as long as we live in these fleshly bodies. The key is to have a "yes" in your heart. In other words, the goal is perfect obedience. We'll never fully achieve it on this side of glory but if we set our hearts to obey and we're quick to repent when we miss the mark, God will honor the intentions of our heart and bless us incrementally as the Holy Spirit continues to shape the character of Christ in us. Make no mistake, this is not a free ticket to sin in the morning and walk in miracles that same afternoon. But you don't have to pay penance, either. The key is genuine repentance. And repentance means changing your mind. Repentance means making a 180-degree turn—moving in the opposite direction of the sin that once held you in bondage.

An Even Better "All Things" Covenant

Fast forward to the New Testament and we find that God has expanded His "all things" promise to include whosoever would believe that Jesus came down from heaven, died on a cross to pay for our sins, rose from the dead in glory and ascended to the right hand of the Father as head of the Church. Not only is this a new covenant, but the Bible calls it a "better covenant on better promises" (Hebrews 8:6).

We already discussed what the Old Covenant offered, which was a boatload of blessings in its own right. What could be better than promises of divine health, financial prosperity, strong relationships and the like? Yet the Word of God says the New Covenant in His blood is better. How could that be possible? Well, for starters, in the New Covenant, there is an exchange. Sins are no longer just forgiven, transgressions are blotted out. We are no longer merely pardoned, we are redeemed. When Jesus died on the cross for us, He set the stage for all things possible.

Jesus talks about the "all things" exchange in Matthew 11:27 (KJV): "All things are delivered unto me of my Father." Jesus also said "The Father loveth the Son, and hath given all things into his hand" (John 3:35 KJV). And again, "All things that the Father hath are mine: therefore said I, that he shall take of mine, and shall shew it unto you" (John 16:15 KJV).

God the Father gave all things into the hand of Jesus. It didn't come cheap for Jesus. He had to pay the price to bring the all things covenant to the world—and He paid it. I've often said that I intend to have everything Jesus died for me to have. If it belongs to me, by golly I want it. And I believe Jesus wants me to have it. Jesus paid for it already. There's no sense in my blessing sitting on a shelf somewhere because I don't believe it's available to me. The same is true for you. Jesus already paid for all things. You can access all things with your persevering faith in His timing.

Before we move on, I want to make sure you really know that all things belong to you spiritually. It's not because of your good works but because of your standing as a disciple of Christ (not as one who merely names Christ among other gods and not as one who is a lukewarm Christian who just seeks blessings without striving for obedience.) Our good works don't qualify us to access all things. Our righteousness is like filthy rags (Isaiah 64:6). But thank God in Christ we have put off our filthy rags, the Lord has clothed us with garments of salvation, and arrayed us with a robe of righteousness (Isaiah 61:10).

Let's look at two more Scriptural witnesses that confirm the all things exchange in our own lives.

> And by him all that believe are justified from all things, from which ye could not be justified by the law of Moses.
>
> Acts 13:39

> Therefore if any man be in Christ, he is a new creature: old things are passed away; behold, all things are become new. And all things are of God, who hath reconciled us to himself by Jesus Christ, and hath given to us the ministry of reconciliation; To wit, that God was in Christ, reconciling the world unto himself, not imputing their trespasses unto them; and hath committed unto us the word of reconciliation.
>
> 2 Corinthians 5:17-19

We are justified in all things. All things are new and all things are of God. If we trust in the living God—and we set our heart to walk in His commandments and we are quick to repent when we slip—He will give us richly all things in His perfect timing (1 Timothy 6:17).

Blessed With Every Spiritual Blessing

Our all things covenant includes every blessing you can imagine—and more. Every area of our lives is blessed, and not just with natural blessings. In Christ, we are blessed with every spiritual blessing in heavenly places (Ephesians 1:3). Our all things covenant includes the blessings of Abraham. But it includes so much more than that. The Israelites weren't partakers of the divine nature. They weren't born again. They didn't have the Holy Ghost dwelling in them to lead them and guide them into all truth.

Now to Him who is able to do exceedingly abundantly above all that we ask or think, according to the power that works in us, to Him be glory in the church by Christ Jesus to all generations, forever and ever. Amen.

Ephesians 3:20-21

I like the way the Amplified translation expounds on this verse: "Now to Him Who, by (in consequence of) the [action of His] power that is at work within us, is able to [carry out His purpose and] do superabundantly, far over and above all that we [dare] ask or think [infinitely beyond our highest prayers, desires, thoughts, hopes, or dreams]…"

In the Old Testament, not one of all things Moses prophesied fell to the ground. Not one good promise God promised by the hand of Moses failed to come to pass (1 Kings 8:56). Again, as Christians, we have the same God and an even better covenant based on better promises.

> But now He has obtained a more excellent ministry, inasmuch as He is also Mediator of a better covenant, which was established on better promises.
>
> Hebrews 8:6

The coming of Christ was a promise. After God fulfilled His promise to send the Christ, the Christ Himself promised to send the Holy Spirit (Luke 24:29). The Holy Spirit is referred to as "the promise" several times in the New Testament. Yes, believers had to wait for the promise, but the promise did not fail (Acts 1:4). We may have to wait until the appointed time for the promise, the miracle, to manifest, but God is never late!

We receive the promise of the Spirit through faith—not doubt, not unbelief, and not works of the flesh—and that's how we receive every promise, every miracle (Galatians 3:14).

> Did you receive the Spirit by the works of the law, or by the hearing of faith? Are you so foolish? Having begun in the Spirit, are you now being made perfect by the flesh?

Galatians 3:2-4

Beyond the Holy Spirit, we have many promises in Christ by the Gospel (Ephesians 3:6). We have the promise of life now and in the age to come (1 Timothy 4:8). We are given exceedingly great and precious promises so that through them we can participate in the divine nature and escape the corruption in the world caused by evil desires (2 Peter 1:4). Consider just a few of God's promises:

> He will supply all your needs according to His riches in glory by Christ Jesus (Philippians 4:19).

> His grace is sufficient for any task (2 Corinthians 12:9).

> We have a way of escape when temptation comes (1 Corinthians 10:3).

> By His stripes, ye are healed (1 Peter 2:24).

> All things work together for good to those
> who love Him and are called according to
> His purpose (Romans 8:28).

All the miraculous promises of God are yes and amen (2 Corinthians 1:20). Of course, those promises aren't merely delivered on a silver platter without any commitment on our part. They are inherited through faith and patience (Hebrews 6:12). The amazingly good news is that God is able to do exceedingly abundantly above all that we ask or think (Ephesians 3:20). Indeed, all things are possible if you believe. Part of developing faith to see the working of miracles in your life is rooting out the lies of the enemy. In the next chapter, we'll look at how the enemy tries to rob us from believing all things are possible in Christ.

Meditation Exercise

I challenge you to dare to ask God for the miraculous. If you can find it in the Word, if it's part of your all things covenant, if God ever did it for anybody ever— dare to ask Him to do it for you. Even if he hasn't done it for anybody—if you need it ask Him! And don't let the devil talk you out of your blessing. Listen to the voice of your God, and don't follow the voice of another.

6

Lies that Rob Your Miracle

Don't let the devil push you around. I said don't let the devil push you around. The devil is like the bully on the playground. He seems bigger than you and he makes scary threats. But he's no match for the Holy Ghost.

When the devil comes with his lies, threats and temptations, tell him your all things covenant includes redemption from the curse of the law, thanks to the blood of Christ. But before you do, make sure you know what you are redeemed from.

If you are ignorant about your redemption, then the devil can deceive you. With that in mind, let's review the curses for disobedience.

> "Cursed shall you be in the city, and cursed shall you be in the country.

"Cursed shall be your basket and your kneading bowl.

"Cursed shall be the fruit of your body and the produce of your land, the increase of your cattle and the offspring of your flocks.

"Cursed shall you be when you come in, and cursed shall you be when you go out.

"The Lord will send on you cursing, confusion, and rebuke in all that you set your hand to do, until you are destroyed and until you perish quickly, because of the wickedness of your doings in which you have forsaken Me.

Deuteronomy 28:6-20

Stop right there. Doesn't this sound like just the opposite of the blessings for obedience? Indeed, it is the opposite. When these things manifest in a believer's life, it's the work of the wicked one. God is not actually sending the curse. Our disbelief—or our disobedience—opens the door to the enemy to work the curse in our life. But our faith and obedience shuts the door on the enemy.

Oral Roberts used to say, "God is a good God and the devil is a bad devil." Jesus had a similar sentiment. Jesus put it this way: "The thief comes only in order to steal and kill and destroy. I came that they may have and enjoy life, and have it in abundance (to the full, till it overflows)" (John 10:10 Amplified).

That should give you a clue: When you face a circumstance that's not in line with the blessings of Abraham—with our all things covenant—arm your mouth with the Word of God, take authority over the curse causeless that's trying to come upon you, remind the devil that the blood of Jesus redeemed you from the curse—and stand in faith believing for your miracle.

By the same token, the enemy doesn't fight fair. Sometimes he attacks even when you are walking in obedience and faith. So, again, if you are seeing the curse of the Law manifest in your life—and if you know you aren't practicing sin—you have the authority to command the enemy to flee in the name of Jesus. And God expects you to. He gave you the authority to enforce His will. He will back you up.

Remember this verse: "The Lord will cause your enemies who rise against you to be defeated before your face; they shall come out against you one way and flee before you seven ways" (Deuteronomy 28:7). Sometimes the Lord will take on the enemy for you as you worship. Other times you need to stand in your authority and command the devil to flee.

Sickness Is Not From God

Let's continue exploring the manifestations of the curse from which we've been redeemed. The next verses have to do with sickness.

The Lord will make the plague cling to you until He has consumed you from the land which you are going to possess. The Lord will strike you with consumption, with fever, with inflammation, with severe burning fever, with the sword, with scorching, and with mildew; they shall pursue you until you perish.

Deuteronomy 28:21-22

Because of these verses, Job's infirmities and even Paul's mysterious thorn in the flesh, many born-again believers think God is the author of sickness. Nothing could be further from the truth.

Entire books have been written to debunk the theological errors that God makes us sick, breaks our legs, or puts cancer on us to teach us a lesson. Much the same, many books have been written to explain the nature of Jehovah Rapha, the God who heals us. I'll sum it up with one verse: "God anointed Jesus of Nazareth with the Holy Spirit and with power, who went about doing good and healing all who were oppressed by the devil, for God was with Him" (Acts 10:38). If God made them sick, then Jesus would have been working against the Father's will by healing them.

I remember when I needed a miraculous healing. I had several "medical conditions" in my physical body that manifested in a string of strange ways. The root of it was a whacked out sympathetic nervous system that caused my heart to beat too fast and my blood pressure to rise up to the point that I would become too dizzy to stand. I was taking medications for this "condition" for which there was no cure, and the medications, of course, caused more unwanted symptoms. I needed a healing. I needed the all things possible covenant to manifest in my life.

When I got saved, someone told me God could heal people. They told me testimonies of seeing limbs grow out of stubs, blind eyes opening, and other miraculous works. They told me of ministers like Benny Hinn and Oral Roberts. They told me healing is for today. I decided to give it a try. (That was my first mistake. You don't give God's Word your best shot. You give it your whole heart.) I asked God to heal me. Nothing happened. I went to the church to have the elders lay hands on me. Nothing happened. I drove 300 miles to attend a healing conference, determined to get my miracle. Nothing happened. (Determination alone won't deliver results. You have to believe from your heart and speak with your mouth over and over again.)

I needed a healing, but all I wound up with was disappointment and that disappointment led me into the death grips of doubt. The devil really had a heyday in my mind. He filled my head with all sorts of doubt; doubts about the truth of healing for today, doubts about God's ability to heal this rare "condition," even doubts about my own salvation.

I got my healing by meditating on what the Word of God says about healing as part of my all things possible covenant. By confessing healing Scriptures out of my very own mouth. By praying in the Spirit to build up my most holy faith. By pleading the blood of Jesus. By thanking God that His Word is true. By faith and patience. And, at the same time, by casting down imaginations when symptoms would arise. By binding up those symptoms in the name of Jesus. By resisting the devil. By fighting the power of doubt and unbelief until the devil got so tired of hearing the truth come out of my mouth that he fled seven ways. Ha! You can do the same.

Break Free From Every Curse!
The curse of the law is downright scary—unless you understand your all things covenant with God. Let's read some more of what we're redeemed from so that the enemy can't trick us into thinking God is the cause of our suffering:

> And your heavens which are over your head shall be bronze, and the earth which is under you shall be iron. The Lord will change the rain of your land to powder and dust; from the heaven it shall come down on you until you are destroyed.
>
> Deuteronomy 28:23-24

Ever feel like your prayers are hitting a bronze sky and falling back down to the ground? Ever feel like you are walking through a spiritual drought? The enemy wants us to feel this way. But we know "if we that if we ask anything according to His will, He hears us. And if we know that He hears us, whatever we ask, we know that we have the petitions that we have asked of Him" (1 John 5:14). We also know that He will never leave us or forsake us (Hebrews 13:5). You may feel dry at times, but He is still there.

> The Lord will cause you to be defeated before your enemies; you shall go out one way against them and flee seven ways before them; and you shall become troublesome to all the kingdoms of the earth. Your carcasses shall be food for all the birds of the air and the beasts of the earth, and no one shall frighten them away.
>
> Deuteronomy 28:25-26

When we are in Christ, we are redeemed from this curse: "Now thanks be to God who always leads us in triumph in Christ, and through us diffuses the fragrance of His knowledge in every place" (2 Corinthians 2:14).

> The Lord will strike you with the boils of Egypt, with tumors, with the scab, and with the itch, from which you cannot be healed. The Lord will strike you with madness and blindness and confusion of heart. And you shall grope at noonday,

as a blind man gropes in darkness; you shall not prosper in your ways; you shall be only oppressed and plundered continually, and no one shall save you.

Deuteronomy 28:28-29

Christ also redeemed us from this curse. We've already established that healing belongs to us. We know that God is not the author of confusion (1 Corinthians 14:33). We know that God has given us a sound mind (2 Timothy 1:7). And we know that He wants us to prosper in all things and be in health, just as our soul prospers (3 John 1:2).

The curse of the law goes on and on. And it would be a frightening passage if we were not in covenant with God. But the God of all things possible has redeemed us from all of these curses—and any other type of curses not listed in this passage. If we are ignorant to our redemption, the enemy can come in like a flood and try to put these things on us. Out of ignorance, sometimes we even receive them. That's why it's so important to know what belongs to you.

Revelation in David's Prayers

When someone is about to leave this world, when their life has come to an end, their last words can take on significance. You've heard the phrase "famous last words." And you've probably heard some famous last words. For example, 16th Century writer Joseph Addison's final words were, "See in what peace a

Christian can die." By contrast, actress Joan Crawford, as her housekeeper began to pray aloud, said, "Don't you dare ask God to help me!" Let's listen in to the last words of King David:

Now these are the last words of David. Thus says David the son of Jesse; Thus says the man raised up on high, the anointed of the God of Jacob, and the sweet psalmist of Israel:

"The Spirit of the Lord spoke by me, and His word was on my tongue. The God of Israel said, the Rock of Israel spoke to me: 'He who rules over men must be just, ruling in the fear of God.

And he shall be like the light of the morning when the sun rises, a morning without clouds, like the tender grass springing out of the earth, by clear shining after rain.'

"Although my house is not so with God, Yet He has made with me an everlasting covenant, ordered in all things and secure. For this is all my salvation and all my desire; Will He not make it increase? But the sons of rebellion shall

all be as thorns thrust away, because they cannot be taken with hands.

2 Samuel 23:1-6

God created all things, but He's not hording it all for Himself and the saints there with him in heaven. All things are not reserved for Abraham, Isaac, Jacob, Peter, Paul and John alone. David understood this. He reverenced God for His power to create all things, and marveled at His willingness to share all things with His creation. David understood his unshakeable "all things" covenant and he walked in it. He understood his salvation. Let's listen to a prayer of David:

> When I consider Your heavens, the work of Your fingers, the moon and the stars, which You have ordained, what is man that You are mindful of him, and the son of man that You visit him? For You have made him a little lower than the angels, and You have crowned him with glory and honor. You have made him to have dominion over the works of Your hands; You have put all things under his feet …
>
> Psalm 8:3-6

David understood that God had a covenant with man that included dominion over all things. He also understood that the Philistines didn't have that same covenant. That's why when the Israelite army shrunk back in fear at the thought of battling Goliath, David ran to the battle line asking, "Who is this uncircumcised Philistine that he should defy the army of the Living God?" (1 Samuel 17:26) David understood his "all things" covenant, and He bet his life on it time and time again. Time and again God showed up to keep His end of the deal. Let's listen to yet another prayer of David:

> Be merciful to me, O God, be merciful to me! For my soul trusts in You; and in the shadow of Your wings I will make my refuge, until these calamities have passed by. I will cry out to God Most High, to God who performs all things for me. He shall send from heaven and save me; He reproaches the one who would swallow me up. Selah. God shall send forth His mercy and His truth.

> Psalm 57: 1-3

Wow. Can you see David's faith? He was in the midst of calamity, but he also knew his God wouldn't let him down. He cried to the God that "performs all things" for him. David knew that God would do whatever was necessary to do to deliver him from the calamity. He knew God would work a miracle! If all things meant parting the River Jordan, David was confident He would do it. If all things meant giving him a divine strategy, David was confident He would do it. David understood that all things are possible to him that believes long before Jesus announced it.

Meditation Exercise

Stop right now and pray. Ask the Holy Spirit to reveal to your heart any area where you have fallen for the lies of the enemy about what's possible in your life. Ask Him to show you any lie that is robbing you of your miracle. Jesus said the Holy Spirit will lead you into all truth (John 16:13). Ask Him to break any deception off your mind and shine the light of truth in your heart.

7

Don't Pervert Your Miraculous Covenant

The Apostle Paul didn't hang out with Jesus in the flesh, but he hung out with the Holy Ghost in the spirit—and he prayed in tongues more than most (1 Corinthians 14:18). So when it comes to understanding (and teaching) God's perspective on our all things possible covenant, Paul is near the top of the go-to list.

Paul received two-thirds of the New Testament by revelation and he wrote plenty about "all things." We'll review some of them in this chapter, beginning with a few words of warning he offered the church at Corinth. The believers there were carnal and were pushing the "all things" covenant to its limits, partaking in "things" that were leading them away from God. Today, we call it the hyper-grace gospel or distorted grace message.

Paul's teaching is simple: Although all things are lawful to believers who have been delivered from the law of sin and death, all things are not beneficial (1 Corinthians 10:23). Paul also said all things are lawful, but all things don't edify. Don't let the devil trick you. God will forgive you for sin if you confess it, but that doesn't give you a license to sin. The gospel of grace is not a cheap patch for lascivious living. Don't abuse the grace of God.

I've included this chapter because we need to have balance in all things. The end of all things is at hand; therefore, be serious and watchful in your prayers (1 Peter 4:7). Be sober, be vigilant; because your adversary, the devil, walks about like a roaring lion, seeking whom he may devour (1 Peter 5:8). When we speak of all things possible, we're talking about activating our covenant with God—not following the devil into excess and extremes. Not sloppy agape. And certainly not the hyper-grace message that's deceiving great numbers in the Body of Christ today.

Your License to Sin? God Forbid!

Are you ready to get real? As believers, we live under the law of liberty, but that doesn't give us a license to sin or to offend others with our liberty. In fact, if we want to enjoy "all things" God has already made provision for, we need to walk circumspectly with Him, not as fools but as wise people (Ephesians 5:15).

www.jenniferleclaire.org

To walk circumspectly means to be careful to consider all circumstances and possible consequences. It may not be a sin to eat a big pork chop, for example, but if it's going to offend your Jewish brother then you why not choose a hamburger instead? Likewise, God won't send you to hell for smoking cigarettes, but it may damage your witness with some or tempt one who is trying to stop smoking. What's more, your body is the temple of the Holy Ghost (1 Corinthians 6:19). Why pollute it?

Walking circumspectly also means considering the consequences of your actions in your own life. It may not be a sin to drink a glass of wine, but what could that one glass of wine lead to? What could it awaken in you? What unwise decisions could it lead you into? It may be lawful—and we won't debate that here—but is it really beneficial? Is it really edifying?

Judging All Things

The Apostle Paul shared some Holy Ghost wisdom in his first epistle to the church at Corinth. "But he who is spiritual judges all things ..." (1 Corinthians 2:15). The Amplified version puts it this way: "The spiritual man tries all things [he examines, investigates, inquires into, questions, and discerns all things]."

Paul put the spiritual man in contrast to the unspiritual man who doesn't welcome God's instruction. What's the lesson here? Before you engage in anything, especially big decisions, be sure to ask God what He thinks about it. That goes for shopping for a new car on Saturday to getting married on Sunday. Like the Preacher said, "In all your ways acknowledge Him, and He shall direct your paths (Proverbs 3:6). Certain activities may not be part of the "all things possible" that God has planned for you at this stage in your life. God's not holding back on you. All things good come to those who wait. You don't need an Ishmael in your life.

Paul continued to drive this point home with his spiritual sons and daughters at Corinth. He said, "All things are lawful for me, but all things are not helpful. All things are lawful for me, but I will not be brought under the power of any" (1 Corinthians 6:12).

Engaging in things that aren't part of God's plan can lead you into bad habits, even addictions, that derail your destiny. Are you getting it? Paul repeated himself later in his letter, determined to make his point: "All things are lawful for me, but not all things are helpful; all things are lawful for me, but not all things edify" (1 Corinthians 10:23). Paul also said, "Test all things; hold fast what is good. Abstain from every form of evil" (1 Thessalonians 5:21-22).

As you judge all things, as you walk circumspectly before the Lord, consider whether the consequences of your behavior are going to make you a slave to sin or build up your spirit. Keep in mind that it was also Paul who said, "Let all things be done for edification." (1 Corinthians 14:26), and again, "Let all things be done decently and in order" (1 Corinthians 14:40). When you tap into all things that God has ordained for you—and when you do it in God's timing, you can be assured of this promise: "God is able to make all grace abound toward you, that you, always having all sufficiency in all things, may have an abundance for every good work" (2 Corinthians 9:8).

The Lovely Truth

Paul was after the truth—no matter what the truth was. Maybe that's one of the reasons he received so much revelation. If you read First and Second Corinthians, you'll see that Paul not only sought the truth for himself, he also sought to help others receive the truth—even when that meant he could be perceived as hard.

Paul was an apostle, and his Christ-given mission was to perfect the saints for the work of the ministry and to build up the Church according to Ephesians 4:11. The end goal of five-fold ministry was, and still is, for believers to come into such unity in the faith and knowledge of Jesus that we will be mature Christians, able to advance God's Kingdom. Paul knew when that happened, we would no longer behave like immature children, being tossed and blown about by every wind of new teaching and being influenced when people try to trick us with lies so clever they sound like the truth.

How did Paul go about reaching this goal? One of his strategies is outlined in Ephesians 4:15 (AMP):

> Rather, let our lives lovingly express truth [in all things, speaking truly, dealing truly, living truly]. Enfolded in

love, let us grow up in every way and in all things into Him Who is the Head, [even] Christ (the Messiah, the Anointed One).

For because of Him the whole body (the church, in all its various parts), closely joined and firmly knit together by the joints and ligaments with which it is supplied, when each part [with power adapted to its need] is working properly [in all its functions], grows to full maturity, building itself up in love.

Ephesians 4:15-16

What is Love?

Love. Everybody wants it. But do we really know what it is? Before we close out this chapter, let's review love. It's important because when we obey the command of love, we'll see all things possible manifest in our lives much more quickly. I submit to you that if you aren't seeing answers to prayer, you may want to examine your love walk.

I want to share with you the Message translation of I Corinthians 13, also known as the "Love Chapter." Sometimes we get too familiar with the King James Version. The Message Bible really shakes this up in a way that should get our attention.

If I speak with human eloquence and angelic ecstasy but don't love, I'm nothing but the creaking of a rusty gate. If I speak God's Word with power, revealing all his mysteries and making everything plain as day, and if I have faith that says to a mountain, "Jump," and it jumps, but I don't love, I'm nothing. If I give everything I own to the poor and even go to the stake to be burned as a martyr, but I don't love, I've gotten nowhere. So, no matter what I say, what I believe, and what I do, I'm bankrupt without love.

Love never gives up. Love cares more for others than for self. Love doesn't want what it doesn't have. Love doesn't strut, Doesn't have a swelled head, Doesn't force itself on others, Isn't always "me first," Doesn't fly off the handle, Doesn't keep score of the sins of others, Doesn't revel when others grovel, Takes pleasure in the flowering of truth, Puts up with anything, Trusts God always, Always looks for the best, Never looks back, But keeps going to the end.

Love never dies. Inspired speech will be over some day; praying in tongues will end; understanding will reach its limit. We know only a portion of the truth, and what we say about God is always incomplete. But when the Complete arrives, our incompletes will be canceled.

Does this sound like you? Are you patient and kind? Are you humble in spirit? Are you forgiving and compassionate? If you want to see all things possible in your life, you need to do all things possible to walk in love. Yes, we all blow it sometimes. When we do, we need to repent and ask the Lord to help us to walk in love. God honors that. But if we aren't making a concerted effort to walk in love—if we are lazy in this area, self-centered, ambitious at the expense of others, jealous and boastful—we may not be ready for all things possible our lives. God can't trust us yet.

Don't shoot the messenger. I'm trying to help you get all things possible and I am just pointing out one of the biggest hindrances to receiving. The Bible says all things that are exposed by light become visible (Ephesians 5:13). Let the Holy Spirit shine a light on your heart, where the love of God is shed abroad (Romans 5:5). You've got the love of God to give. It's up to you to dole it out.

Remember this: Godliness is profitable to all things, having promise of the life that now is, and of that which is to come (1 Timothy 4:8). When you walk in godliness, there is profit. There is profit in the love walk. Those profits, when added to your faith, position you to receive all things possible.

Meditation Exercise

Hyper-grace theology is flooding the Body of Christ in this hour. Some best-selling authors and megachurch pastors are proclaiming this false doctrine. Don't buy into this error. It may sound like it fits into the all things possible covenant, but it is a deceptive thief that will ultimately rob you from your destiny and could leave many outside the Kingdom.

I urge you, by the mercies of God, to reject teachings that distort the gospel. Jesus told us to "Enter by the narrow gate; for wide is the gate and broad is the way that leads to destruction, and there are many who go in by it. Because narrow is the gate and difficult is the way which leads to life, and there are few who find it" (Matthew 7:13-14). The hyper grace message is leading many down a broad path that will lead to destruction if they don't reverse course.

Ask God to give you discernment to recognize false doctrines, which will only continue to spread at a greater pace until Jesus returns.

www.jenniferleclaire.org

8

The Dynamic Duo

Growing up in South during the 1970s and 80s, I believed in Jesus—at least in theory. I remember the painting of The Last Supper hanging in my great grandmother's kitchen. I remember my grandmother reading me passages about how Lot's wife turned into a pillar of salt. As an adult, I even enrolled in a Christian university and wrote papers about various books in the Bible.

But I was still on my way to hell. I was still doing drugs, living with my boyfriend, stealing and otherwise practicing all manner of sin. By the age of 30, I had only darkened the doors of a church a few times in my entire life—mostly for weddings and funerals. Sure, I believed in my head that there was a God. But no one ever presented the gospel to me. I had no understanding of what it meant to be born again until a prison ministry rolled through town while I was incarcerated for a crime I didn't commit. That's when I got desperate enough to seek out the truth.

Let me say it again—I had no understanding. And that lack of understanding could have sent me into a fiery fate for eternity. I learned a valuable lesson through my salvation experience: It's not enough to have head knowledge. It's not enough to know about something. Albert Einstein once said, "Any fool can know. The point is to understand."

Likewise, I barely passed Algebra in high school. I just could not understand it. I sat in class and listened diligently. I could recite the formulas and the rules by heart. But when I tried to apply that knowledge to an equation I came out with the wrong answer almost every time. I had head knowledge but no true understanding.

See, it's not enough to memorize chapter and verse of the Bible. It's not enough to parrot Scripture. Without understanding—and particularly without a Spirit-inspired understanding of what God meant when He said "all things"—we are walking in a measure of deception that dilutes the childlike faith we need to receive the impossible.

The late British author Douglas Adams put it this way: "Don't you understand that we need to be childish in order to understand? Only a child sees things with perfect clarity, because it hasn't developed all those filters which prevent us from seeing things that we don't expect to see."

We should expect to see the impossible in our lives because the all things possible God is our Father. I pray right now that the Holy Spirit will open your understanding that you might comprehend the Scriptures (Luke 24:45).

The Dynamic Duo of
Wisdom and Understanding

If you are a classic comics fan, you are familiar with the Dynamic Duo of Batman and Robin. Indeed, there are many dynamic duos in classic TV Land, from The Lone Ranger and Tonto to Amos and Andy to Timmy and Lassie. But one of the most powerful dynamic duos under the sun is wisdom and understanding. You can find them tag teaming in the Book of Proverbs.

There are 31 chapters in the Book of Proverbs. That means no matter what day of the month it is, you can read a different proverb every day to gain more wisdom and understanding. The Bible has plenty to say about wisdom—and we need to hear it. Consider just how valuable wisdom is in the sight of God.

> For wisdom is better than rubies, and all the things one may desire cannot be compared with her (Proverbs 8:11).

How much better to get wisdom than gold! And to get understanding is to be chosen rather than silver (Proverbs 16:16).

So shall the knowledge of wisdom be to your soul; If you have found it, there is a prospect, and your hope will not be cut off (Proverbs 24:14).

Benjamin Franklin once said, "The doorstep to the temple of wisdom is a knowledge of our own ignorance." That's why we need understanding. For all the Bible says about wisdom, though, it also has plenty to say about understanding. In fact, Solomon, inspired by the Holy Spirit, connected wisdom and understanding over and again. Here are just a few of the many examples:

Happy is the man who finds wisdom, and the man who gains understanding (Proverbs 3:13).

Get wisdom! Get understanding! Do not forget, nor turn away from the words of my mouth (Proverbs 4:5)

He who gets wisdom loves his own soul;
He who keeps understanding will find
good (Proverbs 19:8)

The Bible also says wisdom is before him that has understanding (Proverbs 17:24). Indeed, wisdom and understanding run hand in hand. But remember, it's the wisdom of the Lord we're after, not man's wisdom and not the devil's wisdom. Let's look at a quick comparison:

> Who is wise and understanding among you? Let him show by good conduct that his works are done in the meekness of wisdom. But if you have bitter envy and self-seeking in your hearts, do not boast and lie against the truth. This wisdom does not descend from above, but is earthly, sensual, demonic. For where envy and self-seeking exist, confusion and every evil thing are there. But the wisdom that is from above is first pure, then peaceable, gentle, willing to yield, full of mercy and good fruits, without partiality and without hypocrisy.
>
> James 3:13-18

If we want to position ourselves to receive all things possible from God, we need to seek wisdom and understanding—understanding of His will, understanding of His ways, understanding of our covenant, even understanding of the enemy that comes to rob all things from us. The good news is our "all things" promise list covers that, too. Proverbs 28:5 says, "Evil men do not understand justice, but those who seek the Lord understand all." Hallelujah! When we believe this promise—and act on it through diligently seeking the Lord—one of the rewards we'll find is understanding.

The Spirit and the Word

If you want wisdom and understanding—if you want to activate your faith for all things—you need both the Spirit and the Word. You need the Word of God because it is His express will for your life. But you need the Spirit of God to reveal the Word, to give you a deeper revelation of all things possible, to renew your mind to the miraculous, and to build you up in your most holy faith. When the Word becomes alive in your spirit, faith will rise to meet the anointing and the result is often a miracle. Remember, it is the Lord who gives us the understanding. Our job is to seek it.

When Jesus taught His followers, He often used parables. For example, Jesus once said that the Kingdom of God is like a grain of mustard seed. Those who didn't have spiritual ears—those who weren't hungering and thirsting after righteousness—probably missed His point and missed the blessing that came along with it. But those who pressed in to become true disciples of Jesus received a deeper revelation of the Word. They gained understanding of the mysteries of God. Consider Mark's explanation:

"But without a parable He did not speak to them. And when they were alone, He explained all things to His disciples (Mark 4:34). The Amplified translation says, "He did not tell them anything without a parable; but privately to His disciples (those who were peculiarly His own) He explained everything [fully]."

When you are particularly His own, Jesus, the Word, will reveal Himself to you in a deeper way. He'll expound on all things. And He'll do it by His Holy Spirit.

> But the Helper, the Holy Spirit, whom the Father will send in My name, He will teach you all things, and bring to your remembrance all things that I said to you.
>
> John 14:26

> But God has revealed them to us through His Spirit. For the Spirit searches all things, yes, the deep things of God.
>
> 1 Corinthians 2:10

Paul assured Timothy that if he would consider what he said, the Lord would give him understanding in all things (2 Timothy 2:7). As you read the Word and the many thousands of promises it contains, don't just rush through the verses no matter how familiar you think you are with them. Do what Paul suggested to Timothy: Take some time to consider what the Holy Ghost inspired these men to write. And as you do, ask the Holy Spirit to reveal the Word to you. He won't just give you a parable. He'll give you an understanding of all things that you can bear to hear.

Misunderstanding God's Word

Along the path to understanding, the enemy will try to bring misunderstanding of God's Word—of all things possible—in effort to steal what belongs to you under your miraculous covenant. The enemy is keeping people sick, in poverty, and otherwise deceived by twisting Scriptures, taking verses out of context, blurring the truth, or confusing your mind. Satan is the Father of lies (John 8:44).

The late British poet Lord Alfred Tennyson once said, "A lie that is a half-truth is the darkest of all lies." This is one of Satan's keenest strategies to deceive. He actually uses the truth of Scripture to tempt and trick you. Satan tried this on Jesus after His 40 days in the wilderness:

> Then the devil took him to the holy city and had him stand on the highest point of the temple. "If you are the Son of God," he said, "throw yourself down. For it is written: 'He will command his angels concerning you, and they will lift you up

in their hands, so that you will not strike your foot against a stone.'

Matthew 4:5-6

Jesus didn't fall for Satan's Scripture-twisting, but too often sincere believers do. Sometimes it's plain ignorance of the context. Other times the believers want to believe what the enemy is showing them because it justifies their stance. Still other times, believers are filtering the Word through past experiences or what they have been wrongly taught. And, of course, if we hear the Word and don't do it, we deceive ourselves (James 1:22).

When they fall sick with a cold, cancer or some other ailment, many blood-bought believers are convinced that God has struck them with the infirmity. This is the enemy's lie to rob the word of healing from their heart. Some believers are certain that God burned their house down, tore their marriage up, or brought some other calamity into their lives. This is another lie from Satan. God is a good God and although He may permit the enemy to work in our lives to get our attention when we stray from Him, He also promises to work it for good if we love Him (Romans 8:28). It's tragic when the enemy's lies cause people to get mad at God and turn away from Him so they can't receive His healing, His provision, His restoration and so on.

Meditation Exercise

Nineteenth Century American theologian Tryon Edwards said, "Facts are God's arguments; we should be careful never to misunderstand or pervert them." The enemy tries to pervert God's truth in our hearts so that we'll believe a lie. That's why it's so important to be a student of the Word, but also to learn to rightly divide the Word of truth. Get study guides and commentaries that offer insight into the Hebrew and Greek meanings of words. The Holy Spirit will lead you into all truth (John 16:13) Pray that God would give you wisdom and revelation as you open the Bible.

www.jenniferleclaire.org

9

Can You Believe the Impossible?

Jesus, the one through whom all things were created, had plenty to say about "all things." Jesus is the One who proclaimed all things possible to Him who believes (Mark 9:23). And Jesus is the One who, through His blood, gave us the right to believe for miracles. Thank God for Jesus.

Jesus talked about the concept of "all things" five times in Scripture. If He had said it once, that would have been enough for me. I take Jesus at His word. Yes, it's true that in the mouth of two or three witnesses every word shall be established (2 Corinthians 13:1). Many times, you can find your additional witnesses in the Old Testament. When it comes to "all things," we see these promises since the beginning. But again, Jesus mentions all things five times.

When Jesus repeats Himself, we'd better listen up. He's trying to get a truth over to us that's so important that it becomes a running theme. Love is a Jesus theme. The Holy Spirit is a Jesus theme. Faith is a Jesus theme. And "all things" is a Jesus theme. So without further ado, let's look at what Jesus said about all things.

All Things Are Possible

The first time Jesus mentions "all things possible," it paints a contrasting picture between the inabilities of man and the abilities of God. It positions God as He is—all-powerful. It offers hope and it opens up our eyes to an important Kingdom principle: nothing is too hard for God.

Let's listen in:

> Then Jesus said to His disciples, "Assuredly, I say to you that it is hard for a rich man to enter the kingdom of heaven. And again I say to you, it is easier for a camel to go through the eye of a needle than for a rich man to enter the kingdom of God."
>
> When His disciples heard it, they were greatly astonished, saying, "Who then can be saved?" But Jesus looked at them

and said to them, "With men this is impossible, but with God all things are possible."

Matthew 19:23-26

Here we see the finite mind of man. When the disciples learned how difficult it is for the rich to enter God's Kingdom—the Message translation says it's "easier to gallop a camel through a needle's eye" than for the rich to enter in—they couldn't imagine how anyone could be saved. What imagery Jesus chose to illustrate His point!

Think about it for a minute. Can you imagine trying to gallop a camel through a needle's eye? That is indeed impossible from human terms. There's just no way that's ever going to happen.

With that in mind, consider what Jesus was saying. His point was that it's impossible for a man to save himself—but he has a chance to enter the Kingdom by trusting God to lead him in. Money won't get you into heaven. Works won't get you into heaven. Believing Jesus is the Son of God, was crucified for your sins, died and was raised on the third day is what justifies you.

Praise God! The same God who led you into the Kingdom by faith will lead you into all things possible—if you believe. So let's do ourselves a favor. Let's stop looking at what's possible through our natural eyes and start believing what Jesus said, "With God all things are possible."

All Things, Whatsoever You Ask

Now, Jesus didn't stop by announcing that all things are possible with God. He went a step further to begin teaching His disciples how to access the miraculous. Aren't you glad Jesus let us in on the mysteries of God? If we exercise the Kingdom principles Jesus taught us, we'll access the Kingdom promises God offers us. Let's see what else Jesus said about all things.

> Now in the morning as he returned into the city, he hungered.
>
> And when he saw a fig tree in the way, he came to it, and found nothing thereon, but leaves only, and said unto it, Let no fruit grow on thee henceforward forever. And presently the fig tree withered away.
>
> And when the disciples saw it, they marvelled, saying, How soon is the fig tree withered away!
>
> Jesus answered and said unto them, Verily I say unto you, If ye have faith, and doubt not, ye shall not only do this which is done to the fig tree, but also if ye shall say unto this mountain, Be thou removed, and be thou cast into the sea; it shall be done.

www.jenniferleclaire.org

> And all things, whatsoever ye shall ask
> in prayer, believing, ye shall receive.
>
> Matthew 21:18-22 (KJV)

Again, Jesus speaks of all things being possible. That opens up the realm of the miraculous. He plainly states that if you ask God and believe, you'll receive. The Message translation puts it this way: "Absolutely everything, ranging from small to large, as you make it a part of your believing prayer, gets included as you lay hold of God." And the Amplified translation expresses that whatever you ask for in prayer, having faith and [really] believing, you will receive.

If you aren't seeing all things possible in your life, don't blame God. His Word is true and His promises are yes and amen (2 Corinthians 1:20). It may be that you have to exercise patience with your faith to inherit the promise of God you are waiting to see manifest (Hebrews 6:12). Some things manifest more quickly than others. We have to trust God on the timing. Other times, our faith isn't as pure as we think it is. We aren't really believing with pure faith. I talk about how to cultivate faith that overcomes the world in my book, *Faith Magnified*. If you aren't seeing all things possible in your life, don't get angry with God, yourself or your pastor. Get to the bottom of it with some Holy Ghost wisdom that will help you navigate the spiritual waters on which you are sailing towards the miraculous.

Overcoming Unbelief of All Things

In that vein, let's talk for a minute about all things possible from the perspective of doubt and unbelief. Jesus addressed this ungodly trait in His disciples. You remember the scene. A man brought his demon-thronged son to Jesus' disciples for help. The disciples came up empty in their efforts to cast the devil out.

Jesus called those standing around a "faithless generation." At the very sight of Jesus, the demon threw the boy into a seizure, causing him to writhe on the ground and foam at the mouth. Jesus then addressed the boy's father:

> So He asked his father, "How long has this been happening to him?"
>
> And he said, "From childhood. And often he has thrown him both into the fire and into the water to destroy him. But if You can do anything, have compassion on us and help us."
>
> Jesus said to him, "If you can believe, all things are possible to him who believes."
>
> Immediately the father of the child cried out and said with tears, "Lord, I believe; help my unbelief!"
>
> Mark 9:21-24

Bless this father's heart. He was interceding for his son and he knew it was up to him to believe. He had watched the devil terrorize his boy for many years. When we are in a situation that's been going on for what seems like forever, it can be difficult to believe it's ever going to change. This boy's father was crying out in desperation.

I like how the Message Bible translates Jesus' response to the father. The father asked Jesus, "If you can do anything, do it. Have a heart and help us!" Jesus replied, "If? There are no 'ifs' among believers. Anything can happen." I like that. There are no ifs among believers. Anything can happen because we serve the God of miracles.

I can relate to the father's struggle, though. Remember, he had just been terribly disappointed when the disciples couldn't cast the devil out of the boy. Would he be disappointed again when Jesus commanded the spirits out? The father wasn't completely sure. He believed Jesus could deal with the demons, but unbelief was raging against his weary soul.

Believing After Disappointments

Sometimes when we believe and get disappointed it's harder to muster up faith again. But if we press in, ask God to help our unbelief, and get our eyes back on the Word we can reignite our faith to believe and see miracles even in the face of the most hopeless causes. The father's prayer was answered. Jesus rebuked the unclean spirit that was harassing the boy and he was delivered. When the disciples asked Jesus privately why they couldn't cast out the devil—they had cast out devils before, after all—He said to them, "This kind can come out by nothing but prayer and fasting" (Mark 9:21-29).

I believe Jesus was talking about "this kind" of unbelief. We know that Jesus had given them authority to cast out devils and the disciples had exercised that authority in the past. Once, Jesus sent out 72 disciples and they returned with joy because "Even the demons were subject to us in your name" (Luke 10:17). But somehow the boy with the demon rattled them. Maybe they had never seen such a hard case. Maybe a spirit of unbelief was speaking to the father and the disciples. The father admitted he was struggling with unbelief. Whatever the case, if you can't seem to believe for the miraculous, prayer and fasting could deliver you from unbelief.

Consider this: You can believe with your heart and still battle unbelief in your mind. The key to winning the battle is to continually renew your mind with the Word of God until the Word in you wins out against the unbelief coming against you. In the meantime, cry out to God like this father did. Again, ask God to help your unbelief. Do you know what? He's glad to do it. The Holy Spirit will work with your willing spirit to root the unbelief out so you can have the pure faith to receive your miracle.

The Holy Spirit Helps You

Need a little help learning what belongs to you? The Holy Spirit is your Teacher, your Helper, and your Guide. The Holy Ghost reveals the Word to us. Jesus connected the Holy Ghost to all things possible. The Holy Ghost knows the mind of God on every matter. He is the Third Person of the Trinity. He is part of the Godhead. He is God in action on the earth.

Let's listen in to what Jesus told His disciples about the Holy Ghost in relation to all things possible:

> But the Comforter, which is the Holy Ghost, whom the Father will send in my name, he shall teach you all things, and bring all things to your remembrance, whatsoever I have said unto you.
>
> John 14:26, KJV

The Holy Spirit will teach you all things. What things? Everything you need to know to live as a victorious citizen in the Kingdom of God. Total victory doesn't come overnight and anyone who suggests otherwise isn't being truthful. The Lord drove the enemies out of the Promised Land little by little (Deuteronomy 7:22). But you can have peace even while you are believing for your miracle. And the Spirit of God won't hide any good thing from you. It's part of His mission to help you receive prayer answers (Romans 8:26). The Holy Spirit will grab hold with you in prayer to pull all things possible out of the spirit realm and into your natural life. Thank God for the Holy Spirit! And guess what else? If you forget what belongs to you, He'll even remind you what the Word says (John 14:26).

Before we move on, let's look at this Scripture again in the Amplified translation. I want you to see how important the Holy Spirit is in understanding and obtaining your miracle:

> But the Comforter (Counselor, Helper, Intercessor, Advocate, Strengthener, Standby), the Holy Spirit, Whom the Father will send in My name [in My place, to represent Me and act on My behalf], He will teach you all things. And He will cause you to recall (will remind you of, bring to your remembrance) everything I have told you.
>
> John 14:26 (Amplified)

The Father has sent the Holy Spirit in His name. If you have not received the infilling of the Holy Spirit, there is a prayer later in this book that will help you. Pray in faith and you will receive. Yes, it's just that simple.

The Bible says, "If you then, though you are evil, know how to give good gifts to your children, how much more will your Father in heaven give the Holy Spirit to those who ask him!" (Luke 11:13). The Holy Spirit wants to endue you with power, give you revelation, back up the Word in your life—and help you see and receive all things possible according to God's will.

What a Friend We Have in Jesus

What a friend we have in Jesus, all our sins and griefs to bear. What a privilege to carry everything to God in prayer. You know the song. It's a classic Christian hymn that's been remade over and over again. When we come into the Kingdom of God and we are obedient to the Lord Jesus—if we love God with all of our heart, all of our mind, all of our soul and all of our strength and love our neighbors as ourselves—Jesus calls us friend. Wow.

Jesus is our brother by birthright. God is the Father of us all. But if you have a brother naturally speaking then you know that your brother is not always your friend, too. You can probably count on your brother to stick up for you when the bullies are harassing you on the playground. You may even count on your brother to give you a leg up when you are down financially.

Here's my point: You can expect certain things from your brother because you are family. But just because you are brothers doesn't mean you hang out together on the weekends. Some people grow up and haven't talked to their brothers in months or even years. But when your brother is also your friend, you have even closer fellowship. And when we become friends with Jesus, He shares all things with us.

No longer do I call you servants, for a servant does not know what his master is doing; but I have called you friends, for all things that I heard from My Father I have made known to you.

John 15:15

That's powerful! All things Jesus heard from His Father, He shared with the disciples who walked in faith and obedience. He shared all things with His friends—and He still does. He wants to share the mysteries of the Kingdom of God with you. He wants to tell you the secrets of His heart. He wants to show you all things possible so that by faith and patience you can inherit them.

Meditation Exercise

Oswald Chambers was an early 20th century Scottish Baptist and Holiness Movement evangelist and teacher, best known as the author of the devotional *My Utmost for His Highest*, once said, "The dearest friend on earth is a mere shadow compared to Jesus." The decision you have to make is this: Will you be His friend? Will you remain faithful in the face of temptations and trials that aim to derail you from all things possible Jesus has ordained for you? Take a few minutes to consider Jesus as friend and what He gave up for you. There's nothing He wouldn't do for you.

10

Your Miraculous Authority

I was invited to go on an all-expenses paid press trip to Alaska before heading down to Orlando to serve as a volunteer at a Christian conference. It was a two-week journey full of excitement and a grueling travel schedule that would take me from one end of the U.S. to the other (and perhaps a little beyond).

I was looking forward to the five-star hotels and restaurants, the glacier flying, the snowmobiling and the ice caves, as well as the ministry experience in Orlando. I had never experienced any of this. It was all new and exciting. The adventure was set to start in two days—and then I got one of the nastiest flu bugs you'd ever want to meet.

And I was on my own. I had just moved to southern Alabama at the time and didn't know many people. It was just me, my four-year-old daughter, and an ex-Viet Nam veteran named Mr. Flemming who came to check on me from time to time. I was lying there on the couch sick, disgusted and disappointed, knowing that this flu attack was going to spoil my Alaskan adventure at best and keep me from serving at the conference at worst. Both pictures were grim.

Then my little daughter, Bridgette, came into the living room from her bedroom. She sat on the floor next to me, just staring at me. I felt helpless to care for her and assured her that Mr. Flemming would come by soon to make her dinner. But it wasn't Spaghettios and green beans she was concerned about. It was me.

Child-like Faith Packs Power

Do you want to know what this little child did? She laid hands on me and released a prayer of faith for my healing. She certainly was not an elder in the church and she didn't have any oil to anoint me with, but her prayer offered in faith in the name of the Lord resulted in my healing. Within minutes, I was up and about, with all my strength, caring for my daughter and packing for my trip. When Mr. Flemming got there at dinnertime, all he could do was praise God with us.

Jesus said, "Whoever does not receive the kingdom of God as a little child will by no means enter it" (Mark 10:15). Bridgette had faith for my healing because she went to a Christian pre-school that taught her faith. She didn't try to reason it out in her head. She just believed what the Word of God said on the matter. She worked a miracle.

When she heard it was written about Jesus, "who Himself bore our sins in His own body on the tree, that we, having died to sins, might live for righteousness—by whose stripes you were healed" (1 Peter 2:24) she believed it. When she heard it was written, "Heal the sick, cleanse the lepers, raise the dead, cast out demons …" (Matthew 10:8), she looked for opportunities to do so. When she saw me lying there on the couch, perhaps unable to go on the Alaska press trip, she didn't take thought to the fact that I was pale and perhaps slightly green around the gills. She didn't take thought to the fact that I was vomiting anything I tried to swallow. She took thought to the truth she had learned. Bridgette was moved with compassion, stood in her authority in Christ, and extended her child-like faith. The result: the Kingdom of God manifested.

The moral of the story: Child-like faith packs power—and it doesn't have to come from a child. Child-like faith believes God can do all things possible. Do you have child-like faith? It's not hard to develop. Simply believe what God's Word says. And when anything doesn't line up with the Word, exercise the authority God has given you to bring justice.

Christ's Visible Authority

Our all things possible covenant puts us in a position to govern all things with spiritual authority on this earth. The heaven, even the heavens, are the Lord's: but the earth hath he given to the children of men (Psalm 115:16 KJV). In order to see all things possible manifest in our lives, we need an understanding of Christ's authority and our subsequent authority in Him.

Christ's authority was visible when He preached, when He taught, and most of all, when He healed the sick, cleansed the lepers, cast out demons and otherwise exercised His will over natural elements. People were amazed at His teaching, because He taught them as one who had authority, not as the teachers of the law (Mark 1:22). But they were more amazed when He commanded unclean spirits and they obeyed him (Mark 1:27).

Where did Jesus get this authority? That's what the chief priests and elders wanted to know (Matthew 21:23; Luke 4:36). Of course, Jesus got His authority from God the Father:

> For as the Father has life in Himself, so He has granted the Son to have life in Himself, and has given Him authority to execute judgment also, because He is the Son of Man.
>
> John 5:26-27

You might ask, then, who is the Son of man? Jesus referred to Himself as the Son of man over and again and it caused the Pharisees to show their religious spirit. If you want to understand who the Son of man is, we need to look at the Book of Daniel for a clearer explanation:

I was watching in the night visions, and behold, One like the Son of Man, coming with the clouds of heaven!

He came to the Ancient of Days, and they brought Him near before Him. Then to Him was given dominion and glory and a kingdom, that all peoples, nations, and languages should serve Him.

His dominion is an everlasting dominion, which shall not pass away, and His kingdom the one which shall not be destroyed.

Daniel 7:13-15

Christ's Dominion Over All Things

We see in the Book of Daniel that God gave Christ dominion over all things. At the same time, we see in the Book of Genesis that God delegated dominion over the earth to man (Genesis 1:28). Unfortunately, Adam committed high treason and the devil usurped man's delegated authority. When Christ came, He took back what the devil stole and returned it to man—any man who would believe, that is.

See, the earth always belonged to Christ. All things never stopped belonging to Him. The devil merely took possession through deception in the Garden of Eden. Our faith in Christ breaks that deception, restores our authority on the earth, and spiritually seats us in the heavenly places in Christ.

Christ has never left one stone unturned. When it comes to all things, Christ has it covered from the beginning to the end and throughout all eternity. Christ is the steward of all things possible, which is why He can guarantee repeatedly that all things are possible to those who believe. When we begin to understand Christ, we'll begin to build our faith for all things possible.

> He is the image of the invisible God, the firstborn over all creation. For by him all things were created: things in heaven and on earth, visible and invisible, whether thrones or powers or rulers or authorities; all things were created by him and for him.
>
> He is before all things, and in him all things hold together. And he is the head of the body, the church; he is the beginning and the firstborn from among the dead, so that in everything he might have the supremacy.
>
> Colossians 1:13-18 (NIV)

Christ Fills All Things

Christ didn't just create all things. He isn't just before all things. He's not just holding all things together. He's filling all things. When Jesus ascended on high, He led captivity captive, and gave gifts to men. But before He did that, He descended from the heights of heaven into the depths of the lower parts of the earth.

> He Who descended is the [very] same as He Who also has ascended high above all the heavens, that He [His presence] might fill all things (the whole universe, from the lowest to the highest).
>
> Ephesians 4:10 (AMP)

Christ is everywhere. His presence fills all things. That means the miraculous is within your grasp. If you can just touch the hem of His garment, you can draw from His anointing. An anointing that lifts the burden from your shoulders and destroys the yoke over your life. An anointing that heals your body and your emotions. An anointing that empowers you to be a witness and set others free. Where the anointing meets faith, all things are possible. The miraculous happens!

Christ is Above All Things

Christ didn't just create all things. He isn't just before all things. He's not just holding all things together. He's not just filling all things. Christ is also above all things. We see this theme repeated in Scripture, so it's important that we take the time to gain understanding. Considering our all things possible covenant, pray this prayer based on Ephesians 1:17-23 over yourself right now:

God of our Lord Jesus Christ, the Father of glory, in Jesus' name please give me the spirit of wisdom and revelation in the knowledge of Christ, that the eyes of my understanding may be enlightened; that I may know what is the hope of Your calling, what are the riches of the glory of Your inheritance in the saints, and what is the exceeding greatness of Your power toward us who believe, according to the working of Your mighty power which You worked in Christ when You raised Him from the dead and seated Him at Your right hand in the heavenly places, far above all principality and power and might and dominion, and every name that is named, not only in this age but also in that which is to come. God, You put all things under Christ's feet, and gave Him to be head over all things to the church, which is His body, the fullness of Him who fills all in all. Amen.

If you'll pray that over your life every day, consistently, you will see results. You'll begin to see wisdom and revelation in the knowledge of Christ manifest in your life. You'll begin to understand His power, His position and your position in Him. All things possible will begin to seem more possible to you. You will begin believing for the miraculous!

Before we wrap up our study on the authority and preeminence of Christ, we need to look at one more Scripture. The Bible says Christ must be King and reign until He has put all His enemies under His feet. The last enemy that shall be destroyed is death.

> The last enemy that will be destroyed is death. For "He has put all things under His feet." But when He says "all things are put under Him," it is evident that He who put all things under Him is excepted. Now when all things are made subject to Him, then the Son Himself will also be subject to Him who put all things under Him, that God may be all in all.
>
> 1 Corinthians 15:26-28

In other words, Jesus will one day hand the Kingdom over to the Father, so that the Father may be glorified in the Son. Jesus is a steward of all things possible. The impossible is possible because of the kind intention of the Father's will (Ephesians 1:5). And we receive all things possible with the help of the Holy Spirit. Can you see the Trinity working together, in unison, to give us access to the miraculous?

Meditation Exercise

Some believers don't like it when I teach on the believer's authority. They proclaim that the battle is the Lord's and we need only trust Him. But Jesus offered a parable of the 10 servants, to whom a nobleman distributed talents. In Luke 19:13, the nobleman gave them clear instructions to "occupy till I come."

This parable gives us insight into Jesus' expectation for us to do Kingdom business until He returns. Kingdom business includes enforcing Kingdom rules. Jesus came to destroy the works of the devil (1 John 3:8). But the fact of the matter is the devil, who is called our adversary in Scripture, is still roaming about seeking someone to devour (1 Peter 5:8). It's up to us to engage with the enemy when he comes to devour.

When the enemy comes to rob from you, take a stand like Shammah: "And after him was Shammah the son of Agee the Hararite. The Philistines had gathered together into a troop where there was a piece of ground full of lentils. So the people fled from the Philistines. But he stationed himself in the middle of the field, defended it, and killed the Philistines. So the Lord brought about a great victory" (2 Samuel 23:11).

11

When It's All Your Fault

Have you ever worked with a perfectionist? You've probably met one along the way. The perfectionist wants to do it right or not at all, notices every little mistake and hates making them, won't ask for help because it's perceived as a weakness, is highly aware of the demands of others and, well, you get the idea. I know all about perfectionists because I used to be one. Now, I like to say that I'm a recovering perfectionist.

Noteworthy is the fact that perfectionism is actually a doctrine. I didn't realize that until I did some research on the topic. This doctrine states that the perfection of moral character constitutes a person's highest good. It's a disposition to regard anything short of perfection as unacceptable. We serve a perfect God, one without sin who delivered us from sin. But we're still not perfect—and we never will be so long as we're in this flesh.

The good news is God doesn't demand absolute perfection. When Jesus said "Be ye therefore perfect, even as your Father which is in heaven is perfect" He was speaking about walking in love (Matthew 5:44-48

KJV). So don't get hung up on trying to be perfect while you are in this body of flesh or you may get religious instead. We should strive for maturity. That said, we can be in the perfect will of God (Romans 12:2). We should set our hearts to pursue Christ. When we do, we'll mature in Him and find His perfect will.

Our 'All Things' Responsibilities

Although God doesn't expect us to be perfect in the sense that we never make a mistake—or never sin— He does have expectations of us. If we want to access all things possible, we need to be mindful of God's expectations. We need to have an obedient heart. Just as you wouldn't give a car to a 16-year-old who hasn't demonstrated he's mature enough to drive, God isn't likely to give all things possible to a spiritual baby. It's for our own good.

When you read the Bible, you'll notice that certain promises come with conditions or "ifs." It's possible for you to meet those conditions or God wouldn't have attached a condition to the promise. In fact, there is even a condition on our all things possible covenant: we have to believe it. "For what nation is there so great, who hath God so nigh unto them, as the Lord our God is in all things that we call upon him for?" (Deuteronomy 4:7 KJV)

The Scripture uses the words "all things" in many verses to illustrate God's intolerance for compromise. When God spells out an expectation and tags the words "all things" to it that means He doesn't want to hear any excuses! Of course, none of us are perfect and He will listen to our repentant hearts. But with that in mind, let's examine some of God's expectations.

> And in all things that I have said unto you be circumspect: and make no mention of the name of other gods, neither let it be heard out of thy mouth.

> Exodus 23:13 KJV

God expects us to be dedicated to Him in all things. After all, He saved our lives, gave us His authority, blessed us with every spiritual blessing and so much more. He expects us to be circumspect in all things. Again, to walk circumspectly means to be careful to consider all circumstances and possible consequences. When we do, we won't be as quick to speak or as quick to sin.

Are You Tithing?

One area that few like to talk about is tithing. That's because it can be controversial. Without going tit for tat with Scripture, here's my view: If we could give 10 percent under the law, we should be able to give even more under grace. Yes, I believe it's our responsibility to tithe, and I believe God believes that, too. We see the children of Israel tithing and it was connected to abundance.

As soon as the commandment was circulated, the children of Israel brought in abundance the first fruits of grain and wine, oil and honey, and of all the produce of the field; and they brought in abundantly the tithe of everything.

2 Chronicles 31:5

In New Testament Scripture, we see over and over again that churches gave to various causes. In any case, you should give from your heart. God loves a cheerful giver, not one that has to be cajoled into giving (2 Corinthians 9:7). We also know God expects us to give in the proportion that He blesses us (1 Corinthians 16:1-2). We aren't doing away with the Ten Commandments, so why do away with the tithe? The tithe belongs to God. Of course, paying tithes of mint, anise and cumin isn't an excuse to omit the weightier matters of the law: judgment, mercy and faith (Matthew 23:23). That only makes you legalistic.

Stop Robbing From Me!

Let me share my own experience with tithing. After getting out of jail and losing all my clients in the dot-com crash of 2001—I was hardly the only one who lost their shirts after the bubble burst—I was in dire straits. I had very little cash on hand, save one paycheck I received while I was in jail. I had a three-year-old daughter. I had an old car that was likely to break down at any minute—and eventually did. I relied on food stamps just to put meals on the table as I tried to rebuild a business that had me rolling in the dough before I got saved.

Despite my hardship, I was raised to be a generous person. My grandmother would give you her sofa if she felt like you needed it more than she did. My parents have always reached out to help others who were less fortunate. Well, I was one of the unfortunate ones in 2001 but the values instilled in my upbringing prevailed. I had a roommate who often didn't pay rent, or at least not on time. I didn't push the issue. I let others borrow small amounts of money until their payday—but they never paid me back! I had bills to pay—including a new car my grandfather put in his name after the old one left me stranded on an Interstate with my small child—and I had no idea how I was going to make it all work.

When I picked my toddler up from her Christian pre-school that day, she was excited to share with me what she had learned. She enthusiastically quoted Philippians 4:19, assuring me that, "My God shall supply all your need according to His riches in glory by Christ Jesus." This little one was prophesying to me out of the Word of God. She was so confident in what she was saying that it stirred faith in my heart. Out of the mouths of babes! But nothing changed. I was still down in the dumps with a roommate who wasn't carrying her weight, a new car payment and only a couple of clients. Making matters worse, in the freelance writing business it can take months to get paid for the work you do because the deadlines are months ahead of the print date—and you don't get paid until the print date. And so I continued struggling but I continued letting people borrow money.

After I finally got fed up with allowing people to slide by rent-free and not pay back money they promised to deliver by Friday, I dropped to my knees in front of my old couch. I was angry. I was upset. I was flustered. And I was talking to God a mile a minute, telling Him how it wasn't fair; telling Him how I was trying to help people and they were taking advantage; telling Him how I wasn't going to help people anymore if they were going to just rip me off. I went on and on and concluded my rant with, "I'm tired of these people robbing from me!" After I finally shut up, I heard the still small voice of God say, "Then stop robbing from me."

I had heard of tithing in the church I recently settled into but I didn't truly understand the concept. I knew enough, though, to know what God was saying. I needed to start tithing. I needed to start giving the first 10 percent of my income to God. Here's the Scripture: "Will a man rob God? Yet you have robbed Me! But you say, 'In what way have we robbed You?' In tithes and offerings" (Malachi 3:8).

Tithing was a major step of faith, considering that I was barely making ends meet, even with food stamps. But God was faithful to send a child with a rhema word about what He wanted to do according to Philippians 4:19 and then speak to me directly about what was blocking His provision. I was already giving offerings, albeit small ones, but I made a commitment right then and there to begin tithing.

What I discovered is that God's Word is true in this area. When you tithe, the promise is this:

> Bring all the tithes into the storehouse, that there may be food in My house, and try Me now in this," says the Lord of hosts, "If I will not open for you the windows of heaven and pour out for you such blessing that there will not be room enough to receive it. And I will rebuke the devourer for your sakes, so that he will not destroy the fruit of your ground, nor shall the vine fail to bear fruit for you in the field," says the Lord of hosts; "And all nations will call you blessed, for you will be a delightful land," says the Lord of hosts."
>
> Malachi 3:10-12

I talk more about my miraculous story of riches to rags to riches in my book *Breakthrough!* Suffice it to say that once I started obeying God in this area I started getting new clients. Once I began tithing, people who owed me money started repaying me. Once I stopped robbing God, He began restoring the finances the enemy robbed from me—about $70,000 in legal fees—little by little. In fact, I even got reimbursed more than $2,000 in legal fees from my attorney in a surprise check in the mail just weeks later as a down payment on the restoration. Within a year, the Lord moved me to a new city and showed me an oceanfront condo for rent. When I looked out over the ocean from the balcony, He said, "This is yours." It was a miracle. And that's what the God of all things possible will do when you obey Him and believe His promises—a miracle. Today, I own several condos with beautiful views that I rent out.

Pray, Love Teach

God expects us to give, love, pray and teach. The Apostle Peter said, "And above all things have fervent love for one another, for "love will cover a multitude of sins" (1 Peter 4:8). Peter was talking about the love walk. We know that Jesus gave us one new command: to love one another (John 13:34). When we love one another, all men will know that we are Jesus' disciples (John 13:35).

The Apostle Paul exhorted us "in all things showing yourself to be a pattern of good works; in doctrine showing integrity, reverence, incorruptibility, sound speech that cannot be condemned, that one who is an opponent may be ashamed, having nothing evil to say of you" (Titus 2:7-8). Paul was willing to suffer all things for the Gospel's sake (1 Corinthians 9:12). He's the same guy who said, "Do all things without murmuring and disputings (Philippians 2:14 KJV). God also expects us to teach others about Him and His ways.

Teaching them to observe all things that I have commanded you; and lo, I am with you always, even to the end of the age. Amen.

Matthew 28:20

And God expects us to be relatable. Paul was relatable. He was also one of the most spiritual men we see in the Bible. If you are really close to Jesus, you should be relatable as He was.

To those who are without law, as without law (not being without law toward God, but under law toward Christ), that I might win those who are without law; to the weak I became as weak, that I might win the weak. I have become all things to all men, that I might by all means save some. Now this I do for the gospel's sake, that I may be partaker of it with you.

1 Corinthians 9:21-23

God also expects us to keep our word in all things. The world is watching. Will they see compromised Christians who can't be depended on? Or can they call upon us when they need help, knowing we'll demonstrate the integrity and love of God?

But above all things, my brethren, swear not, neither by heaven, neither by the earth, neither by any other oath: but let your yea be yea; and your nay, nay; lest ye fall into condemnation.

James 5:12 KJV

What If You Make a Mistake?

In seeking balance—and in seeking to expose a way the enemy robs all things possible from us—I want to bring some balance to God's expectations. For all of His expectations, to obey His commands, consider this: God also expects us to make mistakes. In fact, He knew what He was getting into when He saved you. He knew you would stumble and fall. Consider this: A righteous man falls seven times but he gets back up again (Proverbs 24:16.) When you make a mistake get up and run back to God for forgiveness—and wisdom and strength not to do it again.

I learned a lesson about God's grace for folks with sincere hearts who make mistakes in a most unexpected way. Remember the new car my grandfather secured in his name after my old car left me stranded on an Interstate? When you get a new vehicle, you aren't used to operating the windshield wipers, the blinkers—or how hard to push the gas and brakes. It takes a few days to get used to all the new bells and whistles, especially after driving a very old car. That's what happened to me.

I had an assignment in Key West, Fla. for an international newspaper. The new car was right on time because the drive is about 14 hours. I set out on my trip, excited about the opportunity but not so excited about the long drive. I didn't have hotel money, so I needed to make the drive straight through. I guess I pushed the petal a little too close to the metal and the Highway Patrol took exception. I heard sirens. Of course, it terrified me because the last run in I had with a cop left me bruised, confused and falsely accused.

I Was Guilty as Sin

Clearly, I was speeding. I need to pay closer attention to the speedometer. It didn't feel like I was going 10 miles over the limit because the new car experience was so smooth compared to the old car. But I was indeed guilty. The ticket cost about $150, which really hurt at the time because I didn't have an extra $150 to spare. If I did, I would have cut the trip in half and rented a hotel room. I signed for the ticket and went along the highway.

Unfortunately, I didn't learn my lesson. I continued down the highway in my bright shiny new car and my gospel music blaring, just praising and worshipping the Lord when, suddenly, I saw lights flashing again. Another $150 ticket. After that, I drove extra slow which made the trip take much longer than it needed to but I wasn't taking any chances. I went to Key West and completed my assignment and drove back two days later across three states without another ticket. Then it happened. I was on the last road before I reached my house and I heard the dreaded sirens again. I thought surely this kindhearted Southern cop would give me a break but he showed no mercy. He wrote me a $75 ticket.

I didn't know what I would do because I didn't have money to pay all these tickets but I managed to get the money before the deadline. I went on with my life and stayed clear of speeding tickets and police—until I moved back to Florida.

Sure enough, it wasn't long before I got pulled over again. This time, the cop's charges were questionable at best. I was in a school zone and I was very conscious of my speed. I am confident I was not speeding but that didn't matter. According to the police officer, my license had been suspended for the past year. I had absolutely no idea. I never got a letter in the mail. I never got a notice of any kind. I had paid my tickets and moved on. He threatened to take me to jail. When he went back to his car I called a friend to pray. I was terrified that I was about to go back to jail. According to the statutes, it's a criminal offense! The cop could have charged me with a felony. A first time offense can result in 60 days in jail and a fine up to $500.

I Didn't Feel Worthy

I truly had no idea that my license was suspended! Thank God, in His mercy, He touched the heart of this police officer. He answered the prayers. The cop let me go and I went home to deal with the situation. The authorities told me my license would be suspended for a year. I was distraught. How could I possibly go without a license for a year? How would I drive my daughter to school? How would I meet with the many newfound business clients the Lord had brought me?

A close friend of mine tried to build faith in me to believe that God would turn it around, but I wouldn't hear it. I was upset and I didn't think I could ask the Lord to get me out of the situation because, after all, I was the one who was dumb enough to speed three times in a row. My mind was focused on how to solve the problem of not having a license rather than turning to the One who could work a miracle in the situation. Nevertheless, more mature intercessors petitioned God for me and I said a weak "amen."

Much like the men who lowered their friend through a roof to get a healing from Jesus (Mark 2:4), God used faith-filled friends to position me for a miracle. A few weeks later I received a letter in the mail from the State of Florida with a brand spanking new driver license included and a clearance to drive again. Rather than charging me with a misdemeanor or a felony, the state effectively pro-rated the suspension. The state counted the last 12 months that I had been unknowingly driving with a suspended license as the suspension period, reinstated my license and even re-issued new paperwork.

This may seem like a small thing to you, but it was a bona fide miracle in my eyes. And it taught me a great lesson: Even when we mess up—even when the challenge we are facing is totally our fault—we can still run to God to help us fix it. It may not always be wiped completely clean like my driver license situation was. There may be some consequences you have to walk through. I went to driver school one Saturday for eight hours while the case was pending against me, but that was a small price to pay to see a miracle. And it was a miracle. The state didn't have to handle it that way. I broke the law. I was driving with a suspended license, whether I knew it or not. But God responded to my weak "amen" and worked a miracle. How much more can He do with faith that believes for miracles?

Meditation Exercise

If you've made mistakes—and we all have—don't run from God. Run to God. And remember this: "And we know that all things work together for good to those who love God, to those who are the called according to His purpose" (Romans 8:28). God can turn all things around for you. He really can. Just love Him and keep walking in His path and believe Him for the miracle you need. Then stand in faith no matter how long it takes.

Some miracles happen in an instant. Other miracles have to be walked out. Remember, the miracle of a baby takes nine months to birth. Abraham and Sara waited much longer for their miracle baby. Whatever miracle you are believing God for, don't give up just because it doesn't happen overnight or because you've made mistakes along the way. Stay right—or get right—with God and keep believing.

Think right now about the most impossible situation you are facing. Something you never thought would change because it's your fault. Once you've put your finger on it—and it probably won't take long—dare to ask God to help you fix it. Find Scriptures that speak His will over your situation and speak them out of your own mouth. Begin believing God for a miracle!

12

Building Miraculous Faith

N ow faith is the substance of things hoped for, the evidence of things not seen (Hebrews 11:1). The Bible says that by faith the elders obtained a good testimony. Do you want to build a good testimony? The first key to building miraculous faith is to understand that "the worlds were framed by the Word of God, so that the things you see were made of things which are visible" (Hebrews 11:3). God created all things out of nothing by His spoken word. Again, remember, if God doesn't have it He can make it for you.

The so-called Hall of Faith in Hebrews 11 calls out a number of men and women that the Holy Spirit offers up as examples of miraculous faith. By faith, for example, Noah built an ark to escape the flood that wiped out every living thing on the earth. People probably thought he was crazy for believing God but he got his miracle: divine protection. Oftentimes, getting your miracle means ignoring the scoffers and refusing to consider their arguments against your wonder-working faith. When man comes against you for believing the Word, remember that God is with you.

By faith Sarah received strength to conceive a child when she was barren. By faith Abraham was willing to sacrifice that same promised child. Now that's faith! Think about it for a minute. Abraham and Sarah had believed for the miracle of the child Isaac for many years. Once he grew into his teenage years, Abraham believed God would raise him from the dead if he sacrificed him in obedience.

Sometimes God will ask you to make a sacrifice and believe Him for a miracle just to see if you really trust Him. When you are willing, He'll often provide a ram in the bush for you (Genesis 22:13). If He allows you to make the sacrifice, He'll give you something far better in return. God is not going to leave you hanging!

> And what more shall I say? For the time would fail me to tell of Gideon and Barak and Samson and Jephthah, also of David and Samuel and the prophets: who through faith subdued kingdoms, worked righteousness, obtained promises, stopped the mouths of lions, quenched the violence of fire, escaped the edge of

the sword, out of weakness were made strong, became valiant in battle, turned to flight the armies of the aliens. Women received their dead raised to life again.

Others were tortured, not accepting deliverance, that they might obtain a better resurrection. Still others had trial of mockings and scourgings, yes, and of chains and imprisonment. They were stoned, they were sawn in two, were tempted, were slain with the sword. They wandered about in sheepskins and goatskins, being destitute, afflicted, tormented—of whom the world was not worthy. They wandered in deserts and mountains, in dens and caves of the earth.

Hebrews 11:13-16

The Pursuing Kind of Faith

Believing God for the miraculous isn't always an easy road but the only time it's impossible is without faith. That's why the devil wants to rob your faith. He uses smoke and mirrors—people and circumstances—to do it. That's why you can't just seek Him for what He can do for you. You have to seek Him for who He is. And you can't just seek Him when things are going good (or when things are going bad). You have to diligently seek him.

Hebrews 11:6 says, "But without faith it is impossible to please Him, for he who comes to God must believe that He is, and that He is a rewarder of those who diligently seek Him." At this point, you believe in God and you believe He wants to bless you. That puts you in the realm of believing for miracles. But do you diligently seek Him? Or do you just seek Him when it's convenient for your busy schedule? Do you pencil God in and try to seek Him when you can or are you diligently seeking Him? Diligent means steady, earnest and energetic effort. Does that describe your God-seeking? Many times miracles are unexpected. But sometimes miracles demand what I call pursuing faith.

What is the pursuing kind of faith? Pursuing faith is faith that presses in like the woman with the issue of blood. She was plagued with a problem for 12 years and endured plenty of suffering from doctors. She spent all the money she had and got worse instead of better. Maybe you can relate. But then she heard about Jesus.

> She had heard the reports concerning Jesus, and she came up behind Him in the throng and touched His garment, For she kept saying, If I only touch His garments, I shall be restored to health. And immediately her flow of blood was dried up at the source, and [suddenly] she felt in her body that she was healed of her [distressing] ailment.

Mark 5:27-29

The woman with the issue of blood pressed in to God. Mostly likely she had to crawl on the ground under the crowd to reach the hem of His garment. She probably had to combat all manners of imaginations. She even broke the law by coming out of her house in this unclean state. She could have been stoned. But she had pursuing faith that focused on a single goal: receiving her miracle.

God's Word is Our Foundation

The first key to building wonder-working faith is to know what the Word says. It sounds simple, but it's the genesis of the supernatural. God's Word is the foundation upon which we build our faith. If we build our faith in Christ, who is the Word, then we won't be washed up when the rains of trouble come pouring down, or when a flood of trials comes crashing against our soul, or when the winds of tribulation come beating against our life. Put another way, when we know what God's Word says on any given topic we can work with the Holy Spirit to renew our minds with that truth so when the enemy comes whispering his lies we'll flat out reject them before they can take root in our souls.

The soul is a gateway to your spirit man. You hear the Word with your natural ears and read it with your natural eyes. When your soul prospers with the Word of God it causes prosperity in other areas of your life. John called out two aspects of prosperity that faith in the Word brings: "Beloved, I pray that you may prosper in all things and be in health, just as your soul prospers" (3 John 1:2). When your soul prospers with the Word of God, all things become possible.

Even if you're a bit jaded because you've waited and watched others receive miracles while you are doing everything you can to get Gods' attention, I'm here to tell you that your time is coming. It's possible to build faith for all things possible. It's possible to build your faith to receive the miraculous! Faith comes by hearing and hearing and hearing and hearing the Word (Romans 10:17). So listen up, meditate on the truth you read in this chapter, and prepare your heart to see miracles—all things possible—in your life.

Take Baby Steps

We've talked about child-like faith but I want to introduce the concept of baby steps. Whether you are a brand new believer or a seasoned veteran who's met with disappointments over unfulfilled promises—or somewhere in between—taking baby steps is a strategic approach to building faith that works miracles. In other words, work your way up to wonder-working faith. Believe God for what your soul tells you is possible before you believe Him for what your soul tells you is impossible. With a few easy wins under your belt, you can tell your soul to shut up when it rises up in disbelief at the miracle you are believing God for. You can remind yourself of the string of prayer answers you've received and build your faith in the goodness of God before you release your faith for the miraculous.

With this "baby steps" concept in mind, let's do a quick review of some of Jesus' words while He walked the earth. First, He promised us that with God all things are possible (Matthew 19:26). Soon thereafter, He assured us that all things, whatsoever we ask in prayer, believing we shall receive (Matthew 21:22). He also guaranteed all things are possible to him that believes (Mark 9:23).

These are great and precious promises that must not be minimized. Jesus wasn't making promises just so He could take up a big offering at the end of the message. Jesus cannot lie. He is the Truth. When He says it, you can believe it. Jesus said all things are possible. The only catch: We have to believe it.

That said, don't start off trying to believe for all things at once. If your life is a mess, if you have great needs, start by believing God for the most immediate need. Again, build your faith to receive something small before you try to extend your faith for something life-changing. Much like physical strength is built up by first lifting light weights and later lifting heavier weights, faith is built up by believing God first for smaller things and later for bigger things.

Now, I'm not saying that you can't charge out there and believe God right now to fix the biggest problem you've ever faced in the world. I'm just suggesting that if you've struggled to receive in the past, wisdom may dictate nurturing your faith by feeding it smaller victories until it becomes strong enough to overcome the world. You can do all things through Christ who strengthens you (Philippians 4:13).

Faith's Prerequisite

One of faith's prerequisites is believing that God can do it. We know that God is all-powerful and all-knowing. He can do anything. Nothing is too hard for Him (Jeremiah 32:17). He is merciful and gracious, full of wisdom and might. God is able to do exceedingly, abundantly above all that we ask or think, according to the power that works within us (Ephesians 3:20). He is the all-sufficient one. He is the Creator of all things. And remember: If by some chance He doesn't have it, He'll make it for you.

You may not have a hard time believing that God can do anything. But you may have a problem believing He wants to do it for you. Keep this in mind: Romans 8:32 says, "He who did not spare His own Son, but delivered Him up for us all, how shall He not with Him also freely give us all things?"

Think about it for a minute. God delivered up Jesus for you. He already made the ultimate sacrifice for you. He was separated from His Son. He experienced the pain of that separation—and He did it willingly. And if that's not enough, once you receive Jesus by faith He's willing to give you all things possible by faith.

What a God we serve! God is not holding back. That should cause thankfulness to rise up in your heart.

Meditation Exercise

Building miraculous faith starts with a decision and requires determination. Sometimes miracles fall in your lap but most of the time it requires pursuing faith. Take some time to consider what's missing or broken in your life. Which of God promises have eluded you?

Now, decide in your heart in this moment that you will do whatever it takes to see God's best—even miracles—manifest in your life. But don't stop there, put some action behind your decision. Pick up your Bible and find the Scriptures to build your faith for the impossible. Write them out on a piece of paper and keep them in front of your eyes every day. Post them on your refrigerator, put a copy in your car or your purse. Start now!

www.jenniferleclaire.org

13

The Holy Spirit
Unlocks the Miraculous

When I was on the mission fields one summer a wise man said this to me: "For he who speaks in a tongue does not speak to men but to God, for no one understands him; however, in the spirit he speaks mysteries" (1 Corinthians 14:2). He actually called me over and said this to me out of the blue. I wasn't expecting it, but I knew I needed to heed what he was saying. I knew I needed to begin praying in the Spirit much more.

How do miracles happen? It's a mystery, really. No one can explain how blind eyes can suddenly see or how deaf ears can suddenly hear or how cancer suddenly disappears or how limbs suddenly grow back—or even how someone gets born again, gets delivered from depression, loses the taste for drugs, and other miracles. Whether large or small, the dynamics of miracles are a mystery.

When you speak in unknown tongues you are speaking mysteries to God. Could it be possible that some of those mysteries are unlocking miracles? I believe so. When that wise man read 1 Corinthians 14:2 to me on the mission field, he was giving me a key to unlocking the miraculous in my life. I left that encounter praying in the Spirit as much as I possibly could. I prayed and prayed and prayed some more. And I began to see wisdom and revelation open up to me. I began to see miracles take place in my life— doors open that no man could open. It didn't all happen at once. I've diligently prayed in the Spirit— more in some seasons than in others—for years. And I am convinced this has unlocked the miraculous.

> But as it is written: 'Eye has not seen, nor ear heard, Nor have entered into the heart of man the things which God has prepared for those who love Him.' But God has revealed *them* to us through His Spirit. For the Spirit searches all things, yes, the deep things of God. For what man knows the things of a man except the spirit of the man which is in him? Even so no one knows the things of God except the Spirit of God. Now we have received, not the spirit of the world, but

the Spirit who is from God, that we might know the things that have been freely given to us by God.

1 Corinthians 2:9-12

Mistaking Miracles for Coincidence

I've seen supernatural debt cancellation. I've seen God intervene in life and death situations. I've seen God position me in places that only He could and, again, open doors that no man could open. Sometimes what looks like a coincidence is a miracle. Remember, the definition of miracle is "an extraordinary event manifesting divine intervention in human affairs." Here's a little miracle for you:

I once received an e-mail from the producers of Sid Roth's *It's Supernatural* television program. The producer wanted to explore the possibility of having me on a weeklong radio series and then a television broadcast. They ordered several of my books and CDs to review and particularly appreciated one work called *Faith Magnified*. Within weeks, I was flying up to Charlotte to tape a radio broadcast that goes to many nations in the world. I was also collecting large checks from the sale of the books and CDs.

Ironically, I had a brand new book coming out in two months, *The Spiritual Warrior's Guide to Defeating Jezebel*. I figured my publicist had reached out to Sid Roth's ministry to pitch an appearance. But I was wrong. When I saw that Brownsville revivalist Steve Hill, who has imparted much wisdom to me, was on the show a few weeks earlier, I figured he had recommended me. But when I emailed Steve he said he had not mentioned my name to Sid Roth.

Next, I reasoned that it was my exposure through *Charisma* magazine that turned their heads. But I was confused that they chose the *Faith Magnified* book because I am known more widely for my teachings on prophetic ministry and spiritual warfare than faith. In fact, I've written several books on faith despite folks telling me that Kenneth Hagin already said everything there was to say about faith and that faith books don't sell. I wrote faith books despite the naysayers because God put it on my heart to write them. In other words, I wasn't doing it for the money. I was doing it out of obedience.

I finally asked one of the producers how they decided to reach out to me and she said she didn't know. But when I was in Charlotte the truth came out: One of the assistants decided to do a Google search for "Jennifer" and "ministry." Wouldn't you know it, the first result on the Google results was my web site. And, wouldn't you know it, they didn't pick up on my prophetic or warfare books. They picked up on the faith materials that God put on my heart to write despite the naysayers. And I was richly blessed financially because of it. I call that a miracle.

Similarly, I landed my position as an editor at *Charisma* magazine through what looked like a coincidence. I received a stray email from one of the other editors there. I had written on a freelance basis for the magazine for many years, but it was nothing consistent and I didn't know this particular editor. I wrote back, "???" The editor admitted he had written to me by mistake as he was gathering the email addresses of freelancers. The current news editor was moving into a new role and the position was open. He asked me if I was interested.

Of course, I was interested. But I was not willing to relocate. I had just bought a condo and I was finally debt-free. This editor told me it was unlikely that they would hire me to work remotely for such a key position. Long story short, I prayed and God opened that door. Coincidence? No. It was a miracle and I believe ultimately it started by me speaking mysteries to God. It was also God's will. It wasn't me breaking down a door. It was God's plan. I had prayed it out with the help of the Holy Spirit in other tongues—speaking mysteries to God, unknowingly, perhaps for years before it manifested.

When You Don't Know How to Pray

Have you ever felt like you just don't know how to pray? You need a miracle but you don't even know what to ask for, other than, "God, give me a miracle!" There's nothing wrong with that prayer but you might get your miracle faster if you pray in tongues.

> Likewise the Spirit also helps in our weaknesses. For we do not know what we should pray for as we ought, but the Spirit Himself makes intercession for us with groanings which cannot be uttered. Now He who searches the hearts knows

what the mind of the Spirit is, because
He makes intercession for the saints
according to the will of God.

Romans 8:26-27

When your faith is at its weakest point, I recommend praying in the Spirit. If you can muster up enough faith to pray in the Spirit over a matter, the Holy Spirit will partner with you to raise supplications to the Father. We have to do our part—pray in tongues by faith—and He will do His part. Christ is interceding for us in heaven and the Holy Spirit is praying with us on the earth. Why wouldn't we expect a miracle?

In the *Matthew Henry Commentary*, the man of God wrote, "The Spirit, as an enlightening Spirit, teaches us what to pray for, as a sanctifying Spirit works and excites praying graces, as a comforting Spirit silences our fears, and helps us over all our discouragements. The Holy Spirit is the spring of all our desires and breathings towards God."

Praying in the Spirit is praying a perfect prayer to a perfect God. When you pray in the Spirit you are praying a perfect prayer and you can expect a perfect answer. Your mind is unfruitful (1 Corinthians 14:4) but that doesn't matter because it's not your mind that produces the miracle. It is the Spirit of God.

Receiving the Holy Spirit

How can you receive the Holy Spirit? You first have to believe that the Holy Spirit is a gift from God. So let's look at what Jesus said as recorded in John 16:7:

"I tell you the truth; It is expedient for you that I go away: for if I go not away, the Comforter will not come unto you; but if I depart, I will send him unto you."

Did Jesus ever tell a lie? Of course not. Is He waiting for you to manifest perfect behavior before you can be filled with the Holy Spirit? Absolutely not! He wants to fill you with the Holy Spirit so you can be perfected, not because you already are. Much like when you got saved, God didn't expect you to come to His throne all cleaned up to ask forgiveness. He knew you were a mess. He wanted you to come to His throne to find mercy and receive grace to clean up your mess. Now, He wants to fill you with His Spirit so you can walk in His grace, which offers power to overcome any sinful habit.

Jesus said, "If ye then, being evil, know how to give good gifts unto your children: how much more shall your heavenly Father give the Holy Spirit to them that ask him?" (Luke 11:13) If you want to become white hot with passion for the Lord, if you need a spark, if you need to rekindle that love, ask the Lord to fill you to overflowing with His Holy Spirit. Why not pray right now before you move on through the pages of this book?

Pray with me:

Father God, I come to you in the name of Jesus. I thank you that you sent your only begotten Son to save me and I thank you that you desire to fill me with your Holy Spirit. Jesus said, "How much more shall your heavenly Father give the Holy Spirit to those who ask Him."

Right now, I ask you in the name of Jesus to fill me with your Holy Spirit. I receive the indwelling of your Spirit right now and I confess by faith that I am Spirit-filled. I thank you that You have given me a prayer language to communicate with you and I yield my tongue to your Spirit right now. I expect to speak in tongues as the Spirit gives me utterance. I thank you and praise you. Amen!

When you pray in tongues you are doing double duty. Not only are you praying the perfect prayer, thanks to the Helper, you are also building yourself up. Paul and Jude agreed on this. Paul wrote, "He who speaks in a tongue edifies himself" (1 Corinthians 14:4). And Jude wrote, "But you, beloved, building yourselves up on your most holy faith, praying in the Holy Spirit keep yourselves in the love of God, looking for the mercy of our Lord Jesus Christ unto eternal life" (Jude 20).

Meditation Exercise

Do you really know who the Holy Spirit is in your life? Take some time right now to think about who He is. Get out your Bible and do a study if you aren't familiar with the role He plays in your life. The Holy Spirit is always with you. Begin to interact with Him on a daily basis and you will see your spiritual life change. You will grow. He will speak to you and give you revelation. He may be waiting on you to start the conversation.

14

Creating the Impossible
With God's Word

I still have my list of confessions. I've had to print it out more than once over the years because it gets tattered after a while. But these Word-based confessions—when released in pure faith in the power of God—have supernaturally brought the impossible into my life over and over again.

I believe wholeheartedly that it's the combination of praying in the Spirit, as I wrote about in the previous chapter, and confessing the Word that has made all the difference. Praying in tongues or confessing the Word alone is powerful, but combining the two supercharges your faith.

Although I didn't realize it at the time, I discovered the power of confessing all things possible while I was in jail. If you remember my story, when I got a rhema word from Scripture that I would be released on the 40th day I began telling anyone who would listen. I began confessing the will of God over my life even in the face of an impossible situation.

I put my faith on the Word and confessed it as much as I could. And that word came to pass in short order. I was indeed released from jail on the 40th day, despite the natural circumstances that painted an impossible picture. It was a miracle! Of course, God's promises don't always come to pass in 40 days. Sometimes they come to pass much faster. And sometimes we need more patience mixed with our faith to inherit the promises of God (Hebrews 6:12). Just don't stop confessing God's Word.

What Are You Confessing?

I've seen many seemingly impossible things on my confession list come to pass over the years. In my experience, the keys are to make consistent confessions based on God's revealed will and taking action because faith without works is dead. With that said, it's important to note that my faith for "all things possible" undergirded some of my confessions, which were merely desires of my heart rather than the revealed will of God. Let me show you a few examples:

Confession: "I am debt-free." I was anything but debt-free when I began confessing this, but I believed it was the will of God because Romans 13:8 says, "Owe no one anything except to love one another..."

God doesn't want us in debt because the borrower is slave to the lender (Proverbs 22:7). God has given us the power to create wealth (Deuteronomy 8:18). And God wants us to prosper and be in health even as our soul prospers (3 John 1:12). So I confessed I was debt-free even though I had debt upon debt. Today, I am debt-free.

Confession: "My taxes are settled and taxes are not a burden to me." When my husband abandoned our family, he left a large tax bill behind and the IRS was coming after me for the liability because he was in another country. After the trauma of his leaving, the false accusation that landed me in jail, and the life and business rebuilding I went through I fell behind on my taxes. I had a large tax debt and was getting some pretty nasty letters from the government. Today, my taxes are settled and taxes are not a burden to me.

Confession: "I own an ocean-front condo and it is paid for." When I began confessing that, it was purely a desire of my heart. I didn't have a Word of God to stand on, other than Psalm 37:4-5, "Delight yourself also in the Lord, and He shall give you the desires of your heart. Commit your way to the Lord, trust also in Him, and He shall bring it to pass." Today, I not only own a condo that overlooks the ocean with no debt—I paid cash for it—I also own a second condo in North Miami Beach that's paid for and rented out.

I could go on and on. But I think you get the point. This is not a name-it-claim-it, blab-it-grab-it practice. This is not some New Age philosophy or the so-called Law of Attraction. This is me acting like my Father. If Abraham can do it, why can't you?

Therefore it is of faith that it might be according to grace, so that the promise might be sure to all the seed, not only to those who are of the law, but also to those who are of the faith of Abraham, who is the father of us all (as it is written, "I have made you a father of many nations") in the presence of Him whom he believed—God, who gives life to the dead and calls those things which do not exist as though they did; who, contrary to hope, in hope believed, so that he became the father of many nations, according to what was spoken, "So shall your descendants be." And not being weak in faith, he did not consider his own body, already dead (since he was about a hundred years old), and the deadness of Sarah's womb. He did not waver at the promise of God through unbelief, but was strengthened in faith, giving glory to God, and being fully convinced that what He had promised He was also able to perform. And therefore "it was accounted to him for righteousness."

Romans 4:16-22

The kind of faith that brings the impossible into existence is faith that speaks of nonexistent things that

God has foretold and promised as if they already existed (Romans 4:17 AMP). Indeed, the faith that brings the impossible into existence is faith that does not grow weak when you look at your natural circumstances. The kind faith that brings the impossible into existence is faith that doesn't succumb to doubt or unbelief concerning the promise of God. The kind of faith that brings the impossible into existence is faith that gives praise and glory to God before the breakthrough because it believes God is able and mighty to keep His promises. The kind of faith that brings the impossible into existence is faith that understands God created all things—and if He doesn't have it, He'll make it for you.

One more thing: When we confess the Word of God, we're supposed to confess it in faith. There was a time when I was confessing, confessing, and confessing some more when it dawned on me that it would be a waste of time if I wasn't in faith. So I asked the Holy Spirit, "How do I know that I'm in faith?" He answered me quickly: "The very fact that you're confessing the Word demonstrates that you have faith that it will work! If you didn't believe the Word, you wouldn't take the time to confess it all day long!"

Do you get it? It's an act of our faith to confess the Word of God. Then, as we confess the Word of God, faith comes because we hear it. God makes it as easy as He can for us to believe. He even gave us the measure of faith to start off with (Romans 12:3).

The God Who Created All Things

God's Word contains creative power. If you are a born-again believer, you probably don't need to be convinced that God created all things. You already know God created the heavens and the earth. You are sure God created man in His image. You are confident that God created all things through Jesus Christ. I want you to be more convinced, more sure, and more confident because it's vital to your foundation to believe all things are possible to him who believes (Mark 9:23). It's vital to the working of miracles!

If you are going to receive the impossible from God, you need to know He had you in mind when He created all things. You need to know that it's His will for you to enjoy all things He created. And you need to know that "all things" are unlimited. He won't run out before your faith grows enough to receive them. You don't have to be jealous when your neighbor gets the miracle you are believing for. If He's ever done it for anyone, He'll do it for you. And even if He hasn't ever done it for anyone, it's possible for you if you only believe. So let's start building our faith now by reviewing all the things God created.

> In the beginning was the Word, and the Word was with God, and the Word was God. He was in the beginning with God. All things were made through Him, and without Him nothing was made that was made.
>
> John 1:1-3

www.jenniferleclaire.org

John chose the words "all things." But he didn't stop there. Just in case anybody might misunderstand, he added a clause to the end of that statement. He said nothing—not one thing—came into being without Jesus. That's pretty emphatic—and it's absolutely true.

The Apostle Paul put it this way: "To me, who am less than the least of all the saints, this grace was given, that I should preach among the Gentiles the unsearchable riches of Christ, and to make all see what is the fellowship of the mystery, which from the beginning of the ages has been hidden in God who created all things through Jesus Christ..." (Ephesians 3:8-9).

Genesis outlines God's early creations (Genesis 1:1-26). We discover God created everything with His Word. He created light. He created vegetation. He created the sun, the moon and the stars. He created the fish of the sea and every sort of animal. And He created man. He did it all with His Word. This same creative power is within us—if we can believe that all things are possible. Nehemiah had this revelation:

You alone are the Lord;

You have made heaven,

The heaven of heavens, with all their host,

The earth and everything on it,

The seas and all that is in them,

And You preserve them all.

The host of heaven worships You.

Nehemiah 9:6

Nehemiah takes it to the next level. He understood that not only did God create it all—God also preserves it all. That's an important, faith-building revelation. When we receive salvation, we receive so much more than our eternal security. We also receive all things pertaining to life and godliness. That means healing belongs to us, deliverance belongs to us, preservation belongs to us. In fact, the Greek word for salvation implies the ideas of deliverance, safety, preservation, healing and soundness. That's the full Gospel.

Solomon knew that "the Lord has made all for Himself, yes, even the wicked for the day of doom" (Proverbs 16:4). Paul told a council at Athens that "God, who made the world and everything in it, since He is Lord of heaven and earth, does not dwell in temples made with hands. Nor is He worshiped with men's hands, as though He needed anything, since He gives to all life, breath, and all things" (Acts 17:24-25).

Understanding that God created all things, gave life to all things and preserves all things is part of your foundation for believing all things are possible.

Meditation Exercise

Have you ever really heard yourself speak? You could be talking yourself out of your miracle—literally! The words you speak are containers of power. The thoughts you vocalize carry the power of death and life (Proverbs 18:21). Sometimes we develop poor speech habits. We speak out what we see instead of what the Word says. We speak out the doubt the enemy plants in our soul instead of what Scripture echoes in our spirit. Start thinking about what you talk about. Repent of speech that is contrary to God's wonder-working power. And then get your mouth in line with the Word of God.

15

Miraculous Restoration in Your Life

When I was a kid in the 1970s, my parents didn't have a lot of money. My mom decided to stay home with me until I was school-aged, so our family had only one income and the nation was in the midst of what went down in history at that time as the worst recession since the Great Depression. Of course, I had no clue.

Thinking back, though, there were signs that we were struggling along like many young American families of the day. I remember helping my mother roll pennies so we could buy a Christmas tree when I was about four. I also remember my mother using vintage wooden milk crates bookshelves. She was into restoration projects. She could take an old beat up milk crate and turn it into a furniture fashion statement. With some elbow grease and a heavy dose of stain, she could transform something old and worthless into something new and valuable.

That's just what God did with us. When we believed in our hearts and confessed with our mouths that Jesus is Lord, He delivered us from the power of darkness and translated us into the Kingdom of His dear Son (Colossians 1:13). The right to do so belongs to whosoever will...God is no respecter of persons. What's more, "The Lord is not slack concerning his promise, as some men count slackness; but is longsuffering to us-ward, not willing that any should perish, but that all should come to repentance" (2 Peter 3:9). And again, God "desires all men to be saved and to come to the knowledge of the truth" (1 Timothy 2:4).

Greatness in Your Mouth

Of course, we know that all are not saved. Unfortunately, there will be weeping and gnashing of teeth (Luke 13:28). Sadly, some will spend an eternity separated from God. That's why He needs us to get out there and preach the Gospel as if lives depended on it—because lives do depend on it. I was talking with Reinhard Bonnke one time, a German evangelist who has led more than 52 million people to Christ at the time of this writing. He said this to me:

"Anyone who preaches the Gospel has true greatness in their mouth and it's the greatest thing that we could ever speak because it is God's eternal Word which is confirmed as we preach it by the Holy Spirit. I would say to anyone don't be timid. Don't be intimidated. Keep storming the gates of hell. Jesus says unhinge them. And we will plunder hell and populate heaven as we keep preaching the Gospel and bringing those who got saved in contact with Bible-believing churches where they can be nourished and where they themselves can become preachers of the Word of God. I think we often don't like to offend people, but we don't mind offending God. We must preach the Gospel as it is. If we preach what the apostles preach we will get what the apostles got. It is no secret. It is as simple as that."

Another time I was talking to Dr. Myles Munroe, founder, president and senior pastor of Bahamas Faith Ministries International, a network of ministries headquartered in Nassau, Bahamas. He's also authored several books, including *Rediscovering the Kingdom*. I asked Dr. Munroe what God was saying to him about the restoration of the Kingdom of God. And this is what he said:

"We're finally getting to the original message, the original assignment, and the original goal of God. It has always been the restoration of His Kingdom on earth. It is the only message Jesus preached that we can verify. God is restoring the original message of the Bible. This is very significant. It's important to note that Jesus placed the end of the age on the condition that the message of the Kingdom is preached into all the world. I went to college and have a degree in theology, but there was not one class on the Kingdom. I read the four Gospels and it was the only thing that Jesus preached. That was a very strange contradiction to me. The Spirit of God has been speaking about the Kingdom for years, but we are finally listening and that's exciting to me. We will see the true impact of the Kingdom if we keep preaching it."

There's a common string in what Bonnke and Munroe said: We'll see the Kingdom manifesting if we preach the Kingdom. When we preach the Gospel, we will see salvations. We will see change in our society. We will see restoration in families. And we will eventually see the restitution of all things. Christ's willingness to shed His blood and die for the sin of the world made this possible:

For God was pleased to have all his fullness dwell in him, and through him to reconcile to himself all things, whether things on earth or things in heaven, by making peace through his blood, shed on the cross.

Colossians 1:13-21 (NIV)

Thank God for Jesus. God planned for the restoration of all things before the foundation of the world. The Lamb was slain from the foundation of the world (Revelation 13:8). Peter the apostle offers even more insight into God's plan to restore sinful man back to Himself from the beginning.

Knowing that you were not redeemed with corruptible things, like silver or gold, from your aimless conduct received by tradition from your fathers, but with the precious blood of Christ, as of a lamb without blemish and without spot. He indeed was foreordained before the foundation of the world, but was manifest in these last times for you who through Him believe in God, who raised Him from the dead and gave Him glory, so that your faith and hope are in God.

1 Peter 1:18-21

God also prepared a Kingdom for us from the foundation of the world (Matthew 25:34) and chose us in Christ before the foundation of the world, that we should be holy without blame before Him in love (Ephesians 1:4). God is all knowing, all-powerful. God is a God of restoration.

A God of Miraculous Restoration

Yes, God has always been a God of restoration. And when God restores, He restores in abundance. Consider the Old Testament commandments. The Bible says if a man shall steal an ox, or a sheep, and kill it, or sell it he shall restore five oxen for an ox, and four sheep for a sheep (Exodus 22:21). And if the theft be certainly found in his hand alive, whether it be ox, or ass, or sheep, he shall restore double (Exodus 22:4). Exodus and Leviticus are full of such examples.

God is a God of restoration. We also see dead bodies restored to life (2 Kings 8:1). We see lands restored with interest on the fruit of field (2 Kings 8:6). And who could forget the restoration of Job, who received double for his trouble? David spoke of the Lord restoring his soul (Psalm 23:3) and restoring the joy of his salvation after he repented for murder and adultery (Psalm 51:2). Solomon says the thief will restore sevenfold (Proverbs 6:30-32). We see years that were stolen restored (Joel 2:25).

God is a God of restoration and we see the theme continued in the New Testament. We see deformed hands restored to wholeness (Matthew 12:13). We see eyesight restored (Mark 8:25). The Bible says God anointed Jesus of Nazareth with the Holy Ghost and with power: who went about doing good, and healing all that were oppressed of the devil; for God was with Him (Acts 10:38). Jesus was in the business of restoration. He's the one who said, "The thief comes only in order to steal and kill and destroy. I came that they may have and enjoy life, and have it in abundance (to the full, till it overflows)" (John 10:10 AMP).

What Needs Restored in Your Life?

I opened this book talking about my false arrest, my husband abandoning me, then losing all my money and my car breaking down. As I write this book, that was all more than a decade ago. I am here to tell you that God has restored to me all that the enemy stole and then some. Although I can't compare my woes to what Job went through, I can testify to the truth that if you turn to God in the midst of your troubles He will restore what the enemy stole. And He won't just restore it—He'll give you something far greater.

Before I lost it all I thought I had it all, but I had very little. I may have had some cash and a halfway decent car, but I didn't have Jesus. Jesus restored my soul first and then began restoring everything else. My life is truly a miracle. I have more money, more friends, more peace, more joy, more everything than I ever had before I knew Him. He has repaid. He has vindicated. He has brought justice. He has worked miracles—and He is no respecter of persons. If He did it for me, He'll do it for you.

So right now, right where you are, take a few minutes to pray. If you aren't right with God, get right with God. If you've drifted away from Him, run back. If you've been wallowing in self-pity, unforgiveness, bitterness or feelings of unworthiness reject those feelings and embrace God. Nothing is too hard for God. Whatever the enemy has done in your life, it wasn't God's fault. God wants to bring restoration. He wants to resurrect those dead things in your life. All you have to do is believe. It won't happen over night, but it doesn't have to take a lifetime, either. Will you believe the God of miracles?

ABOUT THE AUTHOR

Jennifer LeClaire is a prophetic voice and teacher whose passion is to see the lost come to Christ and equip believers to understand the will and ways of God. She carries a reforming voice that seeks to turn hearts to the Lord and edify the Body of Christ.

Jennifer has a powerful testimony of God's power to set the captives free and claim beauty for ashes. She shares her story with women who need to understand the love and grace of God in a lost and dying world.

Jennifer is the news editor at *Charisma* magazine. She writes a weekly column called "The Plumb Line." Some of her work is archived in the Flower Pentecostal Heritage Museum.

Jennifer is a prolific author who has written several books, including "The Heart of the Prophetic," "A Prophet's Heart," "Doubtless: Faith that Overcomes the World," "Fervent Faith: Discover How a Fervent Spirit is a Defense Against the Devil" and "Breakthrough" Her materials have been translated into Spanish and Korean.

Other Books by Jennifer LeClaire

The Heart of the Prophetic: Keys to flowing in a more powerful prophetic anointing

A Prophet's Heart: Avoiding the Doorway to Deception

Faith Magnified: How to be free from Doubtaholism

Fervent Faith: Discover How a Fervent Spirit is a Defense Against the Devil

Breakthrough!

The Making of a Prophet

The Spiritual Warrior's Guide to Defeating Jezebel

Visit Jennifer online at:

www.jenniferleclaire.org

www.facebook.com/propheticbooks

www.twitter.com/propheticbooks

www.flickr.com/propheticbooks

www.myspace.com/propheticbooks

www.jenniferleclaire.org

CPSIA information can be obtained at www.ICGtesting.com
Printed in the USA
LVOW11s2134190416

484292LV00001B/3/P